AN ILLUSTRATED HISTORY OF MOTORCYCLES

AN ILLUSTRATED HISTORY OF MOTORCYCLES

by
Roy Bacon

ISBN 1 85648 318 5

Publishing Manager *Casey Horton*
Design Manager *Ming Cheung*
Editor *Paul Brewer*
Designer Clear *est* Communications

Printed and bound in Malaysia.

Acknowledgments
The author and the Publisher wish to acknowledge their debt to the many firms and
people who have loaned or given material over the past two decades or more which
has been so useful in preparing this book.
The firms who have obliged at some time over this period include AA, Aermacchi,
Ambassador, Aprilia, Ariel, Batavus, Bavanar, Benelli, BMW, BSA, Cagiva, Can-Am,
Casal, Cooper, Cossack, CZ-Jawa, Derbi, DKW, Ducati, Excelsior, Fantic,
Francis-Barnett, Garelli, Gilera, Gitane, Greeves, Harley-Davidson, Hesketh, Honda,
IFA, Indian, James, Jawa, Kawasaki, Lambretta, Laverda, Maico, Matchless, Meguro,
Mercedes Benz, Mobylette, Morini, Moto Guzzi, MuZ, MV Agusta, MZ, Norton,
Ossa, Piaggio, Progress, Puch, Quasar, Regent, Royal Enfield, Sanglas, Simson,
Suzuki, SWM, Technomoto, Tomos, Triumph, Velocette, Vespa, Vincent-HRD,
Vintage Motorcycle Club, Voskhod, Watsonian, Yamaha and Zundapp,
which makes quite a list.

Friends old and new who have contributed are Paul Adams, Mr Baumann,
Jim Davies, Mike Gardiner, Don Harrell, Tim Holmes, Mr Hunter, Doug Jackson,
Ian Kennedy, John Leathern, Alastair McQuaid, Judy Miedwig, Hans Muller,
Mr Puglisevich, Mr Sadler, Jack Sands, Art Sirota, Sotheby's,
Wm Steele, Stephen Woodhouse.
I hope that I have not missed anyone out; my apologies if I have, it was
not intentional.
Thanks to all who helped.

Roy Bacon

CONTENTS

THE DEVELOPMENT OF THE MOTORCYCLE

THE DEVELOPMENT OF THE MOTORCYCLE

TRIUMPH 1938 SPEED TWIN

PIONEERS
1886-1913

In 1886 Gottlieb Daimler from Germany constructed the first motorcycle powered by a petrol engine. In 1888, Edward Butler from England built a powered tricycle.

The Hildebrand & Wolfmüller motorcycle was produced in 1894 in Germany. This had twin cylinders with the pistons connected to the rear wheel. In England, Colonel Holden built the first four-cylinder machine in 1896. In France the Count de Dion and Georges Bouton combined forces to create the de Dion-Bouton engine, which proved popular with many other companies.

While early machines were unreliable and gave an uncomfortable ride, they offered a special charm, freedom

BUTLER 1884
In Britain, Edward Butler designed the first tricycle, which had twin cylinders connected directly to the rear hub, water cooling and used the two-stroke cycle. Four years later an improved design had a reduction gear and used the four-stroke cycle.

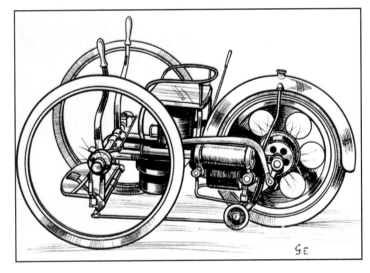

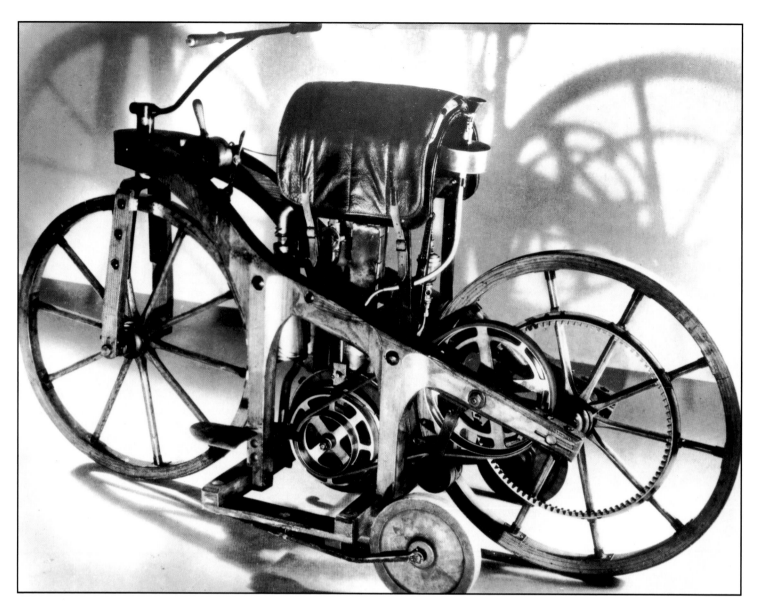

DAIMLER 1885
Gottlieb Daimler designed this wooden-framed motorcycle with an upright engine that drove the rear wheel by belt. The following year he built a version with a countershaft and gear drive.

from the constraints of horse-drawn or public transport and a newfangled adventure. These attributes have remained with the motorcycle to the present day, whether it is used for sport, touring or basic transport.

Until 1896 British motorcycle development stagnated under the law's heavy hand; cars and motorcycles were restricted to a top speed of 6.km/4 miles per hour, and had to be preceded down the road by a man holding a red flag to warn other traffic. This made it virtually impossible to use a powered vehicle. Even after legal changes that year, the pro-horse, anti-motorist theme remained strong. By contrast, in France, Germany and Belgium real progress was made. Their designs forged ahead, although they initially concentrated on the tricycle layout.

By any standards those early machines were very basic. The tricycle was worse, because the engine was positioned behind the rear axle which made them tail heavy. There was a great deal of vibration from the engine and exposed drive gears. The front forks were rigid and the three tracks exacerbated the effects of travelling over rough roads above that of the single track of a two-wheeled motorcycle or the dual tracks of a car. One attempt to avoid this problem was the quadricycle which used four wheels and twin tracks like a car, but was essentially a development of the tricycle adding a front axle to the rear one.

At the beginning of the 20th century the engine position was finally standardised. Up to then it appeared in many locations. Over the front wheel, behind the rear wheel, under the downtube, as the downtube, behind the seat, or built into either the front or rear wheel.

Then, in 1901, Werner Frères of Paris moved their

ACCLES 1896
This Victorian tricycle is typical of British pioneering designs during the late 19th century. It utilised a de Dion type engine from France mounted in front of the rear axle to achieve a good weight distribution.

engine from its original top-heavy mounting above the front wheel to a vertical location within the frame, where it drove the rear wheel by a belt. Pedals for starting the motorcycle went behind the engine and were connected to the rear wheel by the usual cycle chain and freewheel.

The basic layout of the motorcycle was in place. Materials and design still had to be improved, but that engine position dictated that the gearbox, when it came, would fit behind the engine and a two-stage drive should power the rear wheel.

In 1901 the behaviour of metals under the heat and stresses generated in the engine were not understood. Valves and piston rings wore out in a short mileage, lubricating oil gummed the engine when cold and performed badly when hot. The inlet valve was automatic in operation imposing a limit on engine speed and power. Early ignition systems were frail and engine vibration shook most smaller parts loose.

The frame whip was derived from the heavy-duty bicycle so it tended to bend, the rigid front forks would break due to fatigue, the brakes could not reduce speed adequately so riders relied on stout boot soles. In the wet, the

brakes were even worse and the belt that drove the rear wheel would slip on the engine pulley. Belts stretched, their fasteners pulled out and the bicycle-style free-wheel could seize if not frequently cleaned.

Despite the catalogue of problems, the machines generally proved reliable, although most journeys took longer than planned. Delays were normal; but since most riders were young enthusiasts, the problems were overcome. They were tough enough to overlook the hard work and discomfort and to feel challenged by the difficulties. Few women took up motorcycling – they would have to contend with social opprobrium – but there were some prepared to tackle the many problems of riding.

As the decade progressed, technical improvements were made. Mechanically opened inlet valves, Bosch high-tension magnetos and much improved sparking plugs both raised engine speeds and laid most of the ignition troubles to rest. Metals, oils and petrol all became higher quality, spray carburettors were adopted and most machines had mounted lever handlebar controls which made motorcycling easier and safer.

Frames were strengthened and spring front forks

HARLEY-DAVIDSON 1915 MODEL 11F
Technical advances were incorporated in this Harley-Davidson twin-cylinder to complete the basic design of a model produced to the end of the 1920s. It was fitted with an oil pump to replace a drip feed, a three-speed countershaft gearbox in place of the two-speed rear hub, and listed an electric generator rather than acetylene lighting.

became standard – although they did not become universal for some years yet. A few manufacturers offered rear suspension but the systems available proved unpopular, so were seldom seen. Brakes were basic but adequate, except in the wet. Most machines kept the ineffective stirrup front, because the law required motorcycles to have two brakes, and riders were at risk if the front brake worked too well – the wheel might lock and tip them off. At the rear the usual brake was a friction block which was foot operated. Few machines had drum brakes at that time, although they did exist.

It was transmission technology that lagged during those years. The limitations of direct-belt drive with a single ratio and no clutch were soon realised, but the solution was less clear. At first, the engine belt pulley was made adjustable, but this meant the rider had to stop and change the belt length. Acceptable in competition, but hardly

practical for general use. Techniques to adjust the pulley and belt were devised, but they were complex and failed to overcome belt slip in wet weather. Two-speed engine pulleys were tried but wore too quickly. The use of twin chains for alternative ratios was seen as adding expense and weight, which was likely to alienate buyers who preferred the simple designs they knew.

There were many firms who switched their attention to the rear hub and clutch. This could provide three speeds, rather than two. For a while this seemed ideal, but engine power was increasing and V-twin engines were being produced, so the hub gear had to be strengthened. The extra weight soon ruled this out and the ride was described as if the rear tyre was 'stuffed with lead'.

A few firms realised that the countershaft gearbox was the answer to this problem, despite the added expense and the need for the two-stage chain drive. FN in Belgium were already building singles and fours with shaft drive, but these still only had the single speed and most riders viewed the system as being dangerous. The need for the gearbox was emphasised in 1911, when the Isle of Man Tourist Trophy (TT) moved from its original Peel circuit to the 60-km/37-mile Mountain route, with a climb of some 425m/1400 ft. American made Indian motorcycles took the first three places and proved that a gearbox was essential.

All the elements of the modern motorcycle were now in place, although the design was yet to stabilise.

THE GREAT WAR
1914-1918

War frequently forces the pace of technological developments, and the First World War (1914-18) more than most. The advent of an aerial dimension to warfare in the shape of airships and aeroplanes demanded the provision of a reliable power unit. It had to be air cooled to avoid adding the weight of water to that of the rest of the airframe and the risks faced by a fragile cooling system easily put out of action through bullet punctures.

Most of the countries taking part in the war adopted a radial cylinder format for aero engines. Essential research was done on the effects of cylinder heating and the behaviour of the engine's metals. From this came real knowledge of the causes of overheating, distortion and wear. Experimentation led to the discovery of better lubricants, and major advances in materials were made. As a result, a reliable, better-running engine was developed.

This new knowledge was transferred easily from aero to motorcycle engines. In any case, the motorcycle had its own tasks during wartime. All sides found them an essential tool for communications and it quickly displaced the horse, bridging the gaps in telephone networks. Dispatch riders used many different models, although impounded civilian ones proved too frail for the dreadful conditions and the limited attention they could receive.

The British used Triumph singles and Douglas twins, the French kept to their Peugeot, Réné-Gillet and Terrot models, the Italians used Frera or Bianchi models, the Americans kept mainly to Harley-Davidson and Indian, while the Germans had their NSU, Wanderer and Brennabor home-grown makes plus the Austrian Puch. All sides used other makes and models, some impounded, others captured, but any motorcycle that was available and working was pressed into service.

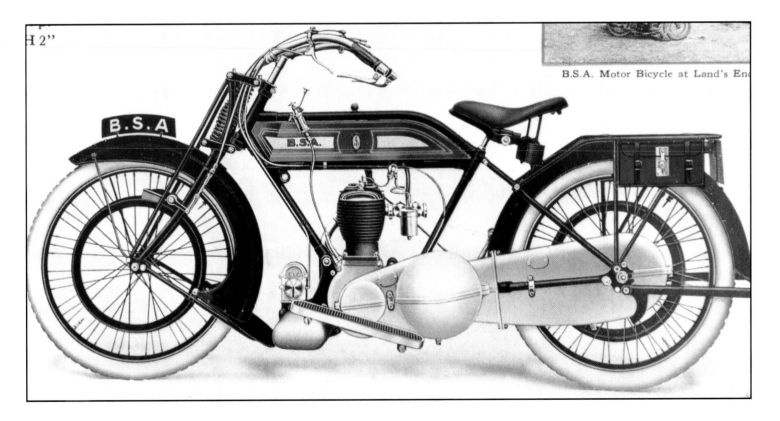

B.S.A. Motor Bicycle at Land's End

BSA 1921
This Birmingham firm built excellent motorcycles at reasonable prices, and ensured that spares were readily available. This was the largest of their singles at the time, here fitted with a three-speed gearbox and cast-alloy chain cases for both sections of the transmission.

DKW 1922 LOMAS
DKW used their existing 143cc two-stroke engine in a scooter layout with such modern features as a pressed-steel frame and pivoted-fork rear suspension. Despite the resulting rider comfort, the machine was costly to produce and soon dropped.

HARLEY-DAVIDSON 1923 MODEL J
The Harley-Davidson Model J of the 1920s included a generator to provide electricity for the ignition and lighting. This fine restoration of an original bike shows the incredible amount of work that goes into such a project, regardless of the type.

Thousands of machines were made for military use, so inevitably, technical developments became limited as the demand for production increased. Races were held at Brooklands in 1915 and some motorcyclists continued to make attempts at breaking records. These were essentially events for the services to act as morale boosters.

The enormous increase in the use of powered transport had a long-term postwar effect. Thousands of young men who previously had little contact with motorcycles were riding, driving and maintaining them. Those who survived the war learned the benefits which personal powered transport would bring.

ROARING TWENTIES
1919-1929

In the years immediately after the war, the motorcycle industry was able to capitalise on the new familiarity with powered transport that the returning men brought home with them. These men and women also recognised that their own car or motorcycle would considerably augment their social life. The conditions for a boom in the manufacture of motorcycles were in place.

In the United States, however, Ford's Model T and the products of other car manufacturers took the largest share of the market for personal transport, leaving the few motorcycle firms to fight for sales to a minority. The main source of business for these firms came from public agencies such as police departments. American motorcycles

had to run on rough roads in harsh weather conditions, and so were built tough, virtually unbreakable.

Compared with Americans, most Europeans found a car too expensive to buy or maintain, so the motorcycle became the favoured purchase, a sidecar added when the family came along. The demand promoted new efforts in design and development, in which Britain took the lead to become the world's major motorcycle manufacturer.

While the demobbed man of 1919 may have been keen to buy, for industry the switch from making war materials to domestic appliances was far from easy, even firms that had been building machines for the services found themselves caught up in a web of acute material shortages, rationing and labour problems.

Around 100 new motorcycle manufacturing firms tried to start up in Britain alone during the first three postwar years. Most bought in nearly all the components they could, but few stayed the course as prices rose dramatically. Order books decreased just as quickly and many small businesses found that they had paid too much, for too little and folded.

Around 1920 the scooter was promoted as the ideal runabout, but it was a short-lived notion. The concept was fine but the results frail, unreliable and impractical. They had a small engine of very limited power which meant that performance was poor and they required the rider to stand on a platform that was unstable and dangerous. Within a couple of years they had gone.

In time, the industry settled down as did the specification of most of its models. The mainstay was the single-cylinder engine, usually of 500cc with side valves, mounted vertically in a frame still displaying bicycle origins. A front-mounted magneto provided the ignition, but was prone to flooding in the wet. The carburettor, which came from a specialist firm, was controlled by twin levers for air and throttle.

The chain-driven gearbox went behind the engine and the clutch was on the mainshaft. Three speeds were the norm although lightweights had two and there were a few machines with four. Gears would be selected through the hand-lever which was tank mounted or bolted directly to the gearbox. Kick-starters and chain final drive systems were becoming common, although belt drive remained for the early part of the decade.

The frame was lower and stronger than a prewar model's. It continued to support the crankcase as before, while its top tubes were now closer together and still housed the tank between them. This was a complex component because it usually had two compartments, one each for petrol and oil. A hand-operated oil pump was mounted on it with a drip-feed sight glass to reassure the rider that the lubricant was flowing through the engine. The shape of the tank was dictated by the twin tubes it lay between and so gave the decade the name 'flat-tank era'.

Front forks were the girder type with single or twin springs, giving some movement and a degree of comfort, although there were steering problems that had to be solved. Speed wobbles were common at the start of the decade but improvements in the forks and damping cured the trouble. Rear suspension remained a rare feature.

Brakes varied. Some models kept the stirrup front and dummy belt rim on the rear wheel purely for the brake. The more advanced models adopted the drum brake, often on the rear wheel with a dummy rim system on the front ones. Drum brakes became the industry standard from the middle of the decade.

Lighting continued to be an added extra. Most riders used the acetylene system, which was a messy process. A carbide generator with rubber pipes was connected directly to the lamps. This system remained in use into the next decade, although electric lighting was available. The problem was the supply of power by dry batteries with their short life, wet batteries that had to be recharged off the machine, or a battery system recharged by a dynamo on the machine. The dynamo system was more convenient, but there were problems matching output to battery capacity; this situation contiued well into the 1930s.

The 500cc single was the basis of most ranges, but there were also many other types. Most firms would offer a similar 350cc, with lighter parts and a larger engine for a sidecar. The V-twin engine became the commonly used power unit for heavy-duty sidecars because it fitted so

HENDERSON 1925 MODEL K
A well-restored example of the Henderson four, connected to sidecar from the same period, for which the owner could specify for an optional reverse gear. Henderson was considered by many to produce the best American fours of the period.

well into the standard motorcycle frame. This was achieved by using two existing cylinders on a new crankcase or by buying the engine from a specialist. Some makers preferred the flat-twin layout with its inherent good balance and a few opted for the vertical twin.

Many small-capacity models were made for the bottom end of the market. Most had a proprietary two-stroke or four-stroke engine under 200cc. European manufacturers produced many ranges of these cheap and simple models because they were often all most people could afford.

In addition, tariffs and other barriers to trade were introduced to protect domestic industries, which had the effect of reducing the choices available to purchasers. This led to firms creating original, cheap motorcycles with high levels of specification, or just some gimmick that caught the public eye. Many of these motorcycles, produced throughout Europe, were kept running for years, because they could be easily maintained and repaired.

The majority of these lightweight machines had simple specifications, but in most cases they had the advantage of a flywheel magneto. This made the costly magneto-and-drive redundant and it was soon easy to add a direct lighting system. In this area the cheaper machine led the way.

There was some innovation, but it was often short-lived, as a result of limited funds or technical inadequacies. Some ideas were radical and worked well, but were not suited to the motorcycle. The radial engine was one such concept; built by Redrup in England, the Radial Three proved how awkward this type of engine was to fit into a standard frame.

The Megola was built in Germany and was stranger still. The five-cylinder radial engine was mounted within the front wheel. Without a clutch or gearbox, the engine was designed to revolve six times faster than the wheel, but in the opposite direction. The machine had a sheet-steel monocoque frame and, despite its odd specification, two thousand were built and some were successfully raced at speeds of up to 144 km/90 miles per hour

Prices decreased as the lessons of mass production were learned, although the effect was less dramatic when compared with the car. Motorcycles could not be as efficiently mass produced at that time and production numbers were smaller. However, where major components were bought in, the benefits accrued and this pulled costs and prices even lower.

British motorcycling teams dominated the road-racing

HARLEY-DAVIDSON 1934 74
The side-valve twin had the more powerful TNT engine fitted, a number of detail changes to both engine and chassis including tail-light, silencer, saddle and fenders, but was otherwise the same as other models produced that year.

scene during this decade, especially the TT, the most prestigious event and comparable with the world title today. They were equally successful in Europe, winning many major events. Off-road their success included winning the International Six Days' Trial Trophy from 1924 to 1929.

Lessons learned from competition were soon applied to the road models. More mmotorcycles were built with overhead valves. Some were given a four-valve layout, but it would take several decades before the benefits of this were fully appreciated. The overhead camshaft was used by only a few, because the extra cost, limited benefit for the engine speeds, and the skill required to assemble and service made it something for the future.

Lubrication systems gradually moved away from constant-loss to dry-sump with a separate oil tank. This removed the need for external oil pipes and made for a neat engine unit. The ignition system was still based on the magneto and the transmission driven by two chains and a gearbox. Some manufacturers offered full chain cases, but most kept the front chain only, while shaft drive was rare. Changing gears continued to be done by hand although many riders bent the lever down so they could kick change the gears. In 1928, Velocette produced the first

positive-stop foot-change system and within a year it was common, although hand changing continued for many years. Frames remained the rigid type, although sheet-steel pressings welded to form the frame appeared in Europe late in the decade. Forks were mainly girder type, although leading-link and trailing-link types were used.

Towards the end of the decade saddle tanks were fitted over the top of rigid frames, increasing capacity and making them more attractive. The tank had to be placed between the upper frame sections on pressed-steel frame models. This marked the end of the flat-tank era. It was also the end of what was later known as the 'Golden Age of Motorcycling'.

DEPRESSED THIRTIES
1930-1939

During the Depression international trade was reduced to a minimum. The motorcycle industry had to cut prices, and this helped persuade some buyers that two wheels

TRIUMPH 1938 SPEED TWIN
Edward Turner was brought into the Triumph firm in 1936 to revitalise it. Late in 1937 he introduced the 499cc Speed Twin model which set the trend for Triumph and the British industry after the Second World War. In time it grew in size and the range was extended, but always kept the original concept of style and performance.

GILERA 1939 WORKS RACER
In 1937 Gilera inherited the CNA Rondine four-cylinder, 500cc racer which had its origins in a 1923 design. It took the chequered flag at Monza that year, dominated the classic races of 1939, and won one race in 1946.

ROYAL ENFIELD 1948 500 TWIN
This Redditch firm adopted two cylinders with this model, which used the same cycle parts as others in the range, but had a new 495cc engine. The gearbox was bolted to the back of the crankcase, a typical Enfield feature, but the ugly front mudguard was soon changed to a more pleasing position.

POWER PAK 1950
Sold from 1950 to 1956, the 49cc Power Pak sat over the bicycle rear wheel with the cylinder hung down on one side and the unit surmounted by the shapely petroil – containing both petrol and oil – tank. Simple to control, it was popular until it was replaced by the moped.

BMW 1951 R51/3
BMW adopted telescopic forks in 1935 and plunger rear suspension in 1938. The twin reappeared in 1950 virtually unchanged. In 1951 the 494cc engine was revised and joined by a 594cc version, the R67. All of the engines produced after the Second World War had overhead valves.

were more affordable than four, if mechanised transport was essential. This was one of the few positive factors for the motorcycle industry during this period.

Pricing was very competitive and brochures were full of low-priced economy machines with minimal specifications. Many optional extras were listed in an effort to entice the buyer into the showroom. Thus, the base model lacked head and rear lamps but the option list provided a choice: the old but cheap acetylene or two types of dynamo system. Tank or machine finish, saddle quality, tank-top instruments, and special tuning were all optional.

In spite of the hard times, technological trends continued to be important. One that ran throughout the decade was the overhead valve engine, fitted with twin-exhaust-port cylinder heads and two exhaust systems, each a chrome-plated pipe and silencer often extended to include a fish-tail outlet clamped to the aft end of the silencer. This trend is unusual not only because of the higher manufacturing cost but also because of the degrading effect of twin ports on performance.

Another trend was to incline the engine and many firms tried this in the early 1930s. It proved a short-lived fad and most manufacturers reverted to the vertical style.

The next innovation was to enclose the bottom section of the engine and the gearbox. This saved money and effort spent on polishing, but proved unpopular so never became a standard feature; it did resurface on particular models from time to time.

In the United States the car was the major form of transport and the number of motorcycle firms was reduced to just two, Indian and Harley-Davidson. In Britain there was a great deal of enterprise from which some progressive models were produced, although development of most of these had been underway prior to the Wall Street Crash in October 1929. The success and survival of new models was always suspect, because the buyer would wait to see how the motorcycle performed, as any problems identified would only be ironed out in the second year of production.

Many British companies either went to the wall in the first half of the decade, or turned their hands to different

INDIAN 1952 CHIEF
In its final form the Chief had a fork cowling and also one to fit to the engine side between the exhaust down pipes, but that is missing from this machine.

AERMACCHI 1957 CHIMERA
The horizontal, single-cylinder engine was this Italian firm's usual style, but this model was enclosed by these stylish panels. It was built in both 175cc and 250cc capacities, but was a poor seller, so it was altered to a conventional layout which sold more successfully.

TOHATSU 1957 PKD-57
Founded in 1922 and a major producer during the late 1950s, this firm concentrated on two-stroke machines such as this 125cc model. Racing versions included a 50cc twin, which appeared in Europe in the early 1960s, but soon after the firm quit the motorcycle business.

products. Others kept themselves going using competitive pricing policies, inspired judgment or just plain good luck. Many firms changed ownership, ranges fluctuated and by 1939 the number of motorcycle manufacturers in Britain had fallen by a third.

There were a few firms that started up production during this period, although many did not survive for long. Some built mainly autocycles – heavy-duty bicycles fitted with 98cc Villiers engines. Proper appreciation of these machines was not to come until the Second World War.

European firms found trade no easier but, in many countries, they were helped because lightweight models were exempt from road tax. Thus in France, Germany and Italy large numbers of small-capacity machines flooded into the home markets.

In Germany, following Adolf Hitler's accession to power, he ordered rationalisation of the industry and the aggressive promotion of German products in competitive events.

Benito Mussolini, the dictator of Italy from 1924, was a keen motorcyclist. Under his patronage Italian firms were encouraged, and technical advances expanded the home market. The Italian passion for racing led to complex and advanced designs making their appearance. Thus, British fans were disappointed in 1935 when Stanley Woods, who had already won the 250cc TT on a Moto Guzzi, triumphed in the Senior race three days later. By 1939 teams from Italian and German factories dominated racing and record-breaking.

Other European countries, less involved in mainstream motorcycling, went through the same economic trauma. Firms in Holland, Belgium, Hungary, Poland and Czechoslovakia all followed the trends when building their products. Many followed the style of the British machines but others went along the pressed-steel frame route which had its own format.

Motorcycles were generally exported from Europe or the United States to the rest of the world. In Japan a few firms produced machines, but those who could afford a motorcycle preferred an import. This was usually an American Harley-Davidson or Indian up to the 1920s when European motorcycles became more popular. Towards the end of that period British machines lost their dominance among Japanese buyers, although this did not have too great an impact since the total market there remained so small. In the 1930s local manufacture increased as a result of military expansion, but production remained low, at just over three thousand machines by 1940.

By the middle of the decade political events in Europe prompted rearmament in many countries and this renewed demand for motorcycles. The improvement in economic conditions encouraged new firms to enter the marketplace, so there was more choice even if many manufacturers used the same components. As profitability rose more enticing features could be incorporated. Improvements were made such as full enclosure of the working engine parts, better control of the electrical generating system and the introduction of rear suspension for more comfortable travel.

The chrome plating which first appeared at the start of the decade began to spread to more parts and there was more use of brighter paint colours.

THE SECOND WORLD WAR
1939-1945

The motorcycle was again an important military tool. Radio communications had taken over from the miles of telephone wire near the front line characteristic of the First World War; but when all else failed, the man on the motorcycle was summoned to deliver the messages.

Motorcycles were commonly used to marshal convoys of vehicles because motorcyclists could direct traffic at one point and then leapfrog ahead, driving along the side of the road, to the next. Motorcycles were also extensively used to scout ahead of advancing troop columns. Some, particularly those coupled with a sidecar, carried weapons, usually either a heavy machine gun or anti-tank weapon.

At the other extreme there were miniatures and lightweights used for training and to carry messages around airfields and army camps. A special type was dropped from aircraft by parachute or in a protective cage. In either case they were used to deploy airborne troops swiftly once they had landed.

Different countries used different types of machine. Most adopted a few basic civilian models, well-developed and easy to service in the field; they removed any inessentials and gave them a military finish.

There were prototypes designed by manufacturers specifically for military use, but only a few of these reached the hands of the troops, because a new design took time to develop and get into production. The development of some new designs took so long that the war was over by the time they were ready. One or two of these models would be put into production after the war, often exported to overseas countries.

Only Belgium and Germany had purpose-built military machines, and one was developed from the other. Belgium's three major firms manufactured massive sidecar outfits to cope with the Flanders mud. The motorcycle was engineered to drive the sidecar wheel for better traction, and it was well endowed with gear ratios to suit all possible needs which included reversing.

The Germans had two firms building machines to the Belgian pattern. These outfits were good in trained hands, but were dangerous to a driver unused to such a sophisticated machine. These were costly to build and demanded high quality materials, which became impossible to obtain as the war continued. By 1944 Germany turned from the sidecar outfits to use the cheap and light solos and their *Kübelwagen*, the equivalent to America's Jeep.

AUSTERE TIMES
1946-1949

After 1945 civilian transport was once again in short supply yet high demand. An immediate answer lay in the enormous numbers of motorcycles no longer needed by the military. Many were sold to dealers, who quickly resprayed them black – service colours being highly

HONDA 1958 SUPERCUB
The most successful vehicle of all time, with sales of over 20 million worldwide. It was built in several sizes from 50cc to 90cc, available everywhere and very reliable. This model was built in 1973, but looks the same as the original, as do those built today.

MZ 1969 ES 150/1
A typical example of the MZ style used by the firm for many years and for several capacities of machines. The sprung front mudguard and cowled headlamp are very characteristic of this manufacturer; nearly half-a-million of these smaller models were produced from 1962 to 1975.

unpopular. Not exciting, but there were many spare parts available, so servicing was not a problem.

This short-term measure filled some needs while industry reorganised for peacetime production. However, material shortages and restrictions affected production.

In Europe, damaged plant, lack of a skilled workforce, economic and political constraints, the major effects of general shortages and millions still under arms hamstrung the industry. Britain had a massive financial debt to pay off so 'export or die' became the call of the day. Most firms simply picked up again on a limited range of their prewar models, the only major change being from girder to telescopic front forks.

Vertical twins were introduced into the ranges of most the major firms, these replacing the prewar V-twins built for heavy-duty sidecars. Sidecar owners used side-valve singles or the new vertical twins although most motorcyclists agreed that the latter were less suited to the combination. Most vertical twins were exported.

In France, the road tax charged on luxury vehicles was very high, so people opted for small-capacity machines –

and that was what was built, although the national flair for style was apparent at motor shows where some larger models were displayed.

Most motorcycle factories in Italy were able to resume civilian production with little delay. There were soon new models and makes. Road-racing machines appeared as quickly, but the major step forward was the scooter, both Vespa and Lambretta models introduced in 1946.

The German industry lay in ruins in 1945 and was at first prohibited from motorcycle production. Then, as the desperate need for transport of any kind became apparent, the prohibition was lifted, although machines were initially restricted to 60cc. This limitation was soon raised to 125cc and then 250cc in 1946. The construction of larger machines was not allowed until November 1949.

In the United States the two remaining firms set out to head off the influx of imports from Britain and Europe. While Harley-Davidson kept to its traditional form of massive V-twin, with one exception, their Indian rival tried to compete head-on with the British vertical twin trend but with little success.

The early postwar years saw many people all over the world use bicycles as the only alternative to walking or public transport. This led to the return to the origins of the motorcycle, an engine attached to a standard bicycle. A host of clip-on units were developed, most of 50cc, driving either wheel by a friction roller. This was especially popular in countries such as Holland, which had a long tradition of cycling. The clip-on unit filled a need for some 10 years before being supplanted by the moped.

There were new designs introduced during the late 1940s. Some were radical and went into production, others did not make it. Most European shows had styling and engineering exercises plus concept models to stimulate development, even if some were too advanced or outrageous to have any hope of being built and sold.

In competitive racing, British factory teams dominated the larger classes and the Italian teams had a grip on the smaller ones. British successes extended world-wide, even to the prestigious Daytona 200 in the United States where Norton won in 1949, the first of four victories. The first world championships were held in 1949 where Les Graham and AJS took the 500cc title, Freddie Frith and his Velocette won all five 350cc races, but Mondial and Moto Guzzi from Italy won the 125cc and 250cc classes. Eric Oliver and his Norton won the sidecar, the first of the four titles this genius on three wheels would take.

Meanwhile, in Japan, the need for any form of private transport was desperate. Alternative forms of transport were at capacity, so to meet the needs of the times, several firms opted to bolt surplus army engines onto bicycles.

One man who travelled this route was Soichiro Honda, but his early efforts were no better than his competitors. However, he was one of the few to improve his product and build his own engine as the surplus army supplies ran out. His motorcycles were to improve dramatically. Compared to what was to come, the production totals in those early years were minute. The Japanese industry output was below the 1940 total of three thousand units right up until 1951, Then it all began to change as the rest of the world concerned itself with home developments.

POSTWAR EXPANSION
1950-1959

The new decade heralded changes and improvements in many countries as wartime regulations finally disappeared, although there were plenty of postwar regulations to replace them. International trade had been re-established and was flourishing, and there was a measure of stability in contrast to the wartime and early-postwar periods. A new era had begun.

This was reflected in the motorcycle industry. There was a move away from the prewar style of motorcycle plus the use of telescopic forks which had served to meet the transport demand. There were some real technical improvements in design, materials, fuels and lubricants. Model ranges increased creating more choice for motorcyclists. New features were added, rear suspension became common and there were more colours used, even if some kept to the traditional black, lined in gold or silver.

The majority of motorcycles were built to a tried and tested format, with either a single or vertical twin cylinder engine. BMW kept to their flat twin used since 1923, and were copied by a number of European firms, although none managed to make them as well. The smaller models were mainly powered by a two-stroke engine but there were a number, many Italian, that used the four-stroke.

It was the manufacture of smaller machines which led to unit construction, with the engine and gearbox built as one, creating models with style. Scooters were developed alongside these small capacity machines and they became a new force on two wheels.

Scooters were a step up in the economic chain of postwar life. In 1945, when few people had powered transport, owning a bicycle was an achievement. For many the first advance possible without great financial strain came when a clip-on unit was bolted to their bicycle. During the 1950s, a way to achieve increased performance from a 50cc engine was found, and the moped replaced the bicycle with a clip-on unit.

The next move for many was either a motorcycle or a scooter. For the enthusiast it had to be the first, but the second appealed to a whole new audience and came close to the 'Universal' model the industry designers had attempted to develop for years. It seemed that there was a vast untapped market for powered transport, which was cheap, easy to park and could thread through traffic.

Many firms attempted to fill this niche. Motorcycles could not, being perceived as noisy, dirty, heavy and awkward to use. The scooter seemed a better alternative, and on tarmac roads it was, thousands turning to it in the 1950s. Off-road, the small wheels of the scooter proved its undoing. In countries where such roads were the norm, the scooter was too expensive. For them, the answer came in 1958 with the Honda Super Cub, a scooterette that combined weather protection and full-sized wheels in a package that millions could afford.

Even though motorcycles and scooters were efficient, fun and exciting forms of transport, they were not really suited to young families. There was a brief period during the late 1950s when this need was partly resolved by the

YAMAHA 1975 DT250
In 1968, Yamaha launched the DT1 into the United States for dirt trail riding. It took elements from motocross and trials models and proved an immediate success because it performed as well on the street as on the trail. It was also available in a range of popular sizes.

bubble car, many of which used motorcycle engines, but this, and the sidecar market, were effectively killed off overnight when the Mini was introduced in 1959.

Most countries went through this cycle from bicycle to car but not at the same time. Thus, the market for any one type changed over the years and successful firms learned to change products to suit demand.

Competition flourished with new motorcyclists becoming household names. On the road racing scene British and Italian men and machines dominated the larger classes, but the Italians kept their grip on the smaller ones except in 1953 and 1954, when the German NSU took the honours. Norton won the sidecar class at first, but eventually BMW took over and began a remarkable domination which was to last for two decades, a phenomenal feat.

In off-road racing, the prestigious International Six Days' Trial was, at first, the property of the British who

won the trophy four times in succession up to 1951. Then, Czechoslovakia took over for the rest of the decade with short interruptions from Britain, East and West Germany. Unlike the British, who stuck to large-capacity four-strokes, the Europeans used small two-strokes developed to be more suitable for the arduous event and its rules.

On the road, motorcycles were refined rather than radically changed and each reflected national trends. The British mainstream was traditional singles, vertical twins, Villiers-powered lightweights and a handful of the unusual models such as the LE Velocette. Germany quickly built up production to become a major force, but peaked in the middle of the decade. Their economic miracle happened quickly and the public en masse deserted two wheels and turned to four.

France concentrated on small machines, such as the *cyclemoteur* which became the moped and continued to

KAWASAKI 1977 Z650
A smaller version of the original Z1 which kept all the features of that motorcycle, but was tuned to give a quicker response. There were also detail changes to suit a smaller capacity engine.

HARLEY-DAVIDSON 1983 SPORT GLIDE
This series, listed as FXR, was launched in 1982. An existing engine and a five-speed gearbox were fitted into a new frame. Despite its name, this model is really a tourer and was soon joined by others in the same series. This is a 1992 machine.

produce a number of larger singles and twin motorcycles. In Belgium it was much the same, and indeed all of the Low Countries used large numbers of light models. Switzerland had a limited home industry but proved a good customer for the other European producers.

In Spain just two firms existed in 1945. But in the 1950s the boom years came. Some three dozen firms were established, many using major components built under licence, yet still made in Spain. Few of these firms were to survive far into the 1960s, but it was an enterprising industry that concentrated on small-capacity, two-stroke models.

The Italians continued to build large and small machines with their own blend of style and flair. Their enthusiasm for any form of powered transport and racing shone through with brilliant engineering and innovative design. Unfortunately, this was all too often allied to poor electrics, bad paint work and peeling chrome, but the package inevitably raised high passions of praise or scorn.

Scooters went from strength to strength during that decade, offering an alternative to the motorcycle that was

not dogged by the outlaw image popularly associated with motorcyclists. Most were built by European firms, apart from British manufacturers who arrived late when the scooter scene had changed. Those who had travelled by Vespa or Lambretta during the decade moved on to a car, but this was not to disrupt scooter sales which were taken over by teenagers in the 1960s.

At the end of the 1950s, the industry had peaked in some countries, but declined in others. Outside Europe there seemed to be little activity. The American industry was reduced to Harley-Davidson, the only major firm and their continued reliance on the V-twin engine, a layout viewed as obsolescent outside the United States.

In Japan, motorcycle designers were looking to Europe for ideas. Many machines made during the 1950s imitated European products. But there was more afoot than copying. Japanese engineers were learning how to build a better motorcycle from the close study of rival products. Such motorcycles as the Suzuki Colleda or Honda CB72 showed that the Japanese students had got their diplomas.

YAMAHA 1986 VIRAGO
This custom model used the air-cooled, V-twin engine concept the firm had first tried five years earlier in a 981cc capacity. The exhausts, low-rider seat, bars and other fittings are all the usual custom items, but final drive was by shaft.

The Japanese also sought publicity for their products. Honda flew a team of riders, machines, spares, mechanics and tools to the Isle of Man for the 1959 125cc TT. The UK press was interested in the Japanese set-up, but had little appreciation of how much had been spent, and subjugated the team to some derision when they were seen to be well off the pace. It was similar to the response Honda received to a 250cc Dream model displayed at the Dutch show earlier that year.

SWINGING SIXTIES
1960-1969

This decade brought many changes to the motorcycle scene and the lead in this came from Japan. This was quite unexpected by the rest of the world, which had little idea of developments in that country.

Japan built a strong industry using a docile home market. By 1960 this was saturated, so they looked to sell their products in Europe and the United States. To meet their needs the Japanese manufacturers had to expand the market by convincing people who would not normally have considered owning a motorcycle to buy one. They achieved this using aggressive advertising campaigns linked to publicity from success in competitions. The whole approach was far removed from the traditional methods of enthusiasts' magazines.

Japan's exotic machines were successful at the races, beginning with the smaller classes in 1961. Ferocious battles between Honda, Yamaha and Suzuki forced the pace of development and produced an era of complex, powerful machines that demanded riders of the highest talent to master them. Only in the 500cc class where MV Agusta hung on, and in the BMW-dominated sidecar class, did the Japanese teams fail. Then, having gained the worldwide publicity they sought, the factory teams withdrew from the Grand Prix scene.

To match the exotic image of racing, the Japanese firms offered sophisticated road models to the general public. In the late 1950s Honda introduced the Super Cub scooterette which became a true machine for the masses and went on to sell over 20 million worldwide. Honda and the other Japanese manufacturers, concentrated on small-capacity machines during the early years, seeking to establish a broad commercial base for later developments.

Some countries used tarriffs and quotas to keep the Japanese imports out, while their own industries maintained output – but with little change or development. Italy, Germany, France and Spain continued to produce the same type of motorcycle, which worked in a limited market, but the sales volumes of these gave little encouragement or finance for anything more radical.

In Britain, the advent of the Mini had already pronounced sentence on the sidecar and the bubble car, both of which faded from sight. Motorcycles moved away from a late-1950s trend of trying to enclose parts of the motorcycle and towards the stark 'café racer' format, while scooters became a teenage fad. This split led to the infamous mods and rocker gangs, which did nothing to promote the use of motorcycles.

The size of the British home market gradually declined, to a third of its best year of 1959. Firms which had built small-capacity models using two-stroke engines, folded or merged one by one. Eventually, the British gave up the bottom end of the market, preferring to concentrate on making large-capacity twins, most of which were exported to the United States.

America went through a boom period in the mid-1960s, partly because of Japanese advertising and also as a result of the advent of trail riding. For this, firms offered street scrambler models, adapted from stock road motorcycles to work well off-road and on trails.

Again, it was the Japanese companies that excelled in this market area, because their light machines were easy for the average rider to handle on the trail. If there were any riding problems, they were seldom serious, and the American countryside offered plenty of vast tracts of open space and spectacular views well worth riding out to.

The British manufacturers offered trail versions of their twins, but these were heavier and harder to ride off-road without some degree of skill. Both on and off the road, those in charge of the British firms thought the Japanese could recruit new riders to the fold with small machines, so that later they would progress to the larger British ones. There was also a belief that the Japanese could not build large motorcycles.

This thinking was incorrect. In many cases, riders who did progress to larger British machines were often disappointed with what they found. They had started on well-finished, fully equipped machines boasting electric start, turn signals and a high standard of reliability. Those they moved on to lacked all these specifications, and in most cases the owner did not appreciate the advantages of finer handling and better brakes.

Then the bubble burst. The warning shot came in 1965 when Honda introduced their Black Bomber 450cc twin offering sophisticated specifications and capacity. Next came the T500 Suzuki in 1967, putting to shame the myth that a large-capacity, two-stroke twin was unreliable. The T500 proved to be reliable, even in the hottest climates such as Death Valley in the United States.

The final blow to the theory that Japanese firms could not build a decent rival to the large British motorcycles came in 1968 when Honda unveiled the CB750. For the first time an overhead camshaft four with electric start and a disc front brake was mass-produced and sold in large numbers. It was an immediate success, while for

HONDA 1986 CN250
A radical scooter, sold as the Helix in the United States, that used laid-back styling for a feet-forward riding stance, a 244cc single-cylinder, water-cooled, overhead-camshaft engine, automatic transmission and provided ample storage space.

those who showed disdain for such luxury, Kawasaki launched the dynamic 500cc triple, a machine of raw power, twitchy handling and great excitement.

Yamaha alone did not offer this type of machine, but their success came with the TD1 production racer, launched in 1962. This 250cc twin-cylinder, two-stroke proved fast from the start, even if fragile at first with poor handling. By 1970 it was quicker, no longer frail, handled well, dominated racing and won the world title.

The European industry progressed little in this decade. The British industry was reduced to just nine firms. Some showed the way forward through specialisation. They produced small numbers of machines for particular sections of sport. Elsewhere, BMW in Germany and Ducati in Italy were poised to introduce exciting new models, the Spanish had discovered the trials machine market and Eastern Europe continued to produce basic models.

In the United States Harley-Davidson acquired a 50 per cent interest in Aermacchi of Italy to provide small-capacity models for the American market. In 1969 Harley-Davidson were bought by American Machine Foundary (AMF). Aside from this they continued with their traditional V-twins mainly produced for the home market.

EASTERN DOMINANCE
1970-1984

By the end of the 1960s the Japanese had achieved their marketing objectives. Their motorcycles were world renowned. They no longer needed to run the exciting, if expensive, racing teams, although the controlling body changed the rules to restrict the specifications and the costs of competing. Thus, the fabulous, complex engines of the late 1960s could no longer be used and the firms turned their energies into using their expertise in the design of more production models.

Motorcycles for the 1970s had to meet new demands as more countries developed their major roads. In the United States highways had always been long and straight, but around the world new motorway construction was bypassing towns far more than it had done in the past. Therefore engines had to be able to run faster for longer, stops depended on the need to refuel or rider fatigue and straight-line speed became paramount.

The easy answer to this need was more power from larger engines, but this brought handling problems. Engineering that was excellent for 50hp with narrow tyres found it could not contain 80hp or more even with added grip from advanced tyre compounds.

There were also problems in stopping as a result of the stainless-steel brake discs, which did not work well in the rain. American riders liked the stainless steel, because it kept its shine and they preferred not to travel in the wet. In Europe, the weather was less obliging and many riders had heart-stopping moments as they waited for the brakes to work; in time the problem was solved.

Large engines, especially the two-strokes, used more fuel, some just 32 km/20 miles for 4.5 litres/1 gallon. Four-stroke machines were more economical, but the more powerful machines could hardly improve on 62 km per litre/40 miles per gallon. The main reason for this was not the high cruising speeds, but the acceleration. It was considered a motorcyclist's prerogative to change down and speed past lines of traffic, but it consumed large amounts of fuel.

Then came the increase in fuel prices and suddenly the world became energy conscious. At this time traffic congestion in cities worsened so millions were faced with tedious, time consuming journeys. Public transport was already packed to bursting point, so some realised that the motorcycle could be the answer.

The word soon spread. Motorcycles were described as cheap, economic, clean, easy to park and socially acceptable. Now the motorcyclist was viewed as someone with a social conscience, who reduced emissions, took up less space in traffic and when parking, who kept the car for family use and weekends. Once seen as an odd person, now they were seen as forward thinking, efficient with time and fuel – someone to emulate. Thousands did and motorcycling had another boom period.

The new market was made up of people who mostly bought small-capacity models. These were usually Japanese, which had adequate town performance, were economical and easy to handle. Mopeds also sold well and motorcycling became a far more respectable activity than it had been in the past.

This massive business expansion enabled the major firms to develop large-capacity models and the 1970s presented a stream of ever-more exotic machines to the public. This culminated in the Universal Japanese Machine, or UJM, which had a transverse four-cylinder, four-stroke engine, twin-overhead camshafts, five or six speeds, twin front discs, electric start and excellent reliability. The root of its faults lay in its weight which did nothing for the handling, wet-weather braking and the way its expensive exhaust system would corrode quickly.

Europe tried hard to fight back. By the 1970s the British industry was in a terminal condition, yet could still build fine motorcycles. From Germany a new BMW range was produced which transformed that company's staid motorcycle image and introduced a trend setting model during the decade. Italy continued to produce many small machines for the home market, but added some larger models which were to become classics.

Most major manufacturers, including those in the United States, continued with traditional lines even if these had to sell alongside the Japanese, who had begun to invest in factories all over the world to avoid any import tariffs or restrictions.

Road racing brightened up from the doldrums of the late 1960s and by the mid 1970s the works machines were back. They all used two-stroke engines despite the efforts of MV Agusta in the 500cc class. From this, the production racers from Suzuki and Yamaha emerged to fill the grids at most events, while American riders made their successful entrance on the Grand Prix circuit.

Transatlantic visits became common from the beginning of the decade, with Europeans riding at Daytona and Americans visiting Britain for a match race series. In time this trend was established, especially when the Japanese works teams reappeared and competed on both sides of the Atlantic in grand prix and endurance racing.

During the decade the Japanese became involved with off-road competitions and soon dominated much of this sport. They surpassed the Spanish, whose industry had excelled at this – but who declined from the middle of the decade both on and off the road. In motocross, the European firms offered fierce competition, so the Japanese had to fight hard for their successes.

The decade ended on a high note with sales up and the industry confident. Further developments made the machines even more sophisticated and handling problems became a thing of the past. However, the economic recession of the early 1980s cut into sales and the motorcycle boom gradually died away. The market for new riders slumped and existing demand was satisfied. Some people moved back to the car, having changed their commuting pattern and become used to higher petrol prices.

All these factors led to another metamorphosis for the motorcycle market. Although machines were already being built to meet the needs of specific groups of purchasers, there were more changes still to come.

CLASSICS TO RETROS
1985-1995

During the 1980s the market for new motorcycles decreased dramatically. Machines became ever more complex and aimed at specific rider groups. But at the start of the decade came an outburst of interest in older machines and the classic bike era was born, the success story of the

1980s. It was part of a new pattern as motorcycling became a leisure activity, something for weekends and holidays.

There were working motorcycles, those used by dispatch riders who carried urgent mail around town and between cities. What began in Britain as an emergency measure to combat a postal strike became an industry, a sure means of establishing a motorcycle's quality.

There had always been interest in older machines, but this had concentrated on the pre-1915 pioneer and pre-1931 vintage models. The new wave of interest was in motorcycles built from the 1930s to the 1960s. People wanted to recapture their youth and sought out either the model they had, or the unaffordable one they had wanted.

In general, it was British machines that were in

KAWASAKI 1988 ZX-10
This motorcycle was at the forefront of machines with the engine housed within an aluminium perimeter frame, which was stronger and lighter than the old type and thereby improving perfomance.

demand. Not for all, as there were enthusiasts for machines from many different countries and some enjoyed the challenge of finding the most obscure. Quickly, the needs of these new collectors became services and a whole restoration industry grew. Some of this was fostered by the recession, as skilled craftsmen, former employees of big firms, found themselves redundant with payments large enough to set up small businesses. Others were already obliging friends by working in their own time, and soon realised that there was enough demand to work in this new industry permanently.

While the classic industry grew, sales of the new machines suffered. Products became more specialised with the accent on sport and leisure riding, so even small-capacity models were designed to conform to range themes.

One of the themes was the race replica, the first of which was introduced in the mid 1980s. More technical advances were made, top-of-the-range models were built with four-valve engines, water cooling and full fairings. The frame and suspension systems adopted the sophistication of the works racing machines and their styling.

This trend became more noticeable as racing moved away from grand prix to competitions based around production models. In turn this led to street-legal production-racer motorcycles listed for sale so owners could enter these races. Some may have been used as sports machines but manufacturers usually offered a replica which looked the same but was marginally adjusted for road use.

Another trend from the mid-1980s was the large-capacity trail model. Small trail machines had been produced for many years, most for gentle off-road use, a few developed and tuned for endurance events, but then they were built larger and powered by four-stroke engines. The trail model, with either single-cylinder or twin-cylinder engine, designer style, graphics and finish were as important as the race replica.

They had a tall static seat, because of the immense movements by the rear wheel suspension, and many saw no more off-road use than the four-wheeled equivalent. However, they were popular and were strong enough to go almost anywhere. Their off-road tyres might have limited their cruising speed to around 145 km/90 miles per hour, but for most owners this was satisfactory.

As the 1990s drew near, manufacturers, influenced by the popularity of classic motorcycles, introduced the retro style. This took a modern engine and gearbox unit and housed it in a chassis copied from the early 1970s. Even Harley-Davidson extended their range through the 1980s

HARLEY-DAVIDSON 1991 ELECTRA GLIDE CLASSIC
Comfort on three wheels at Daytona, this sidecar is finished to match the motorcycle. Such outfits are often seen with the entire catalogue of optional extras, which includes a trailer and paddock bike.

MZ 1995 SKORPION TOUR
Designed by Seymour-Powell, this flagship model of the revived firm is fitted with a five-valve Yamaha single-cylinder engine within a highly-distinctive frame. The touring version has upright bars, the sports one has clip-ons, sports seat, rear-sets and cockpit fairing.

to cover owners' wishes and generate new interest by developing a number of these retro bikes. These new models appeared original, but they incorporated fully modernised equipment.

No other firm chose to go that far in recreating a famous past, although the Japanese manufacturers offered some Harley-Davidson clones. These models used a lookalike of the American machine's narrow-angle V-twin engine, but failed to capture the Harley mystique.

In Britain, Triumph was relaunched but Norton collapsed, while in Italy Ducati went from strength to strength and Aprilla emerged as a major company. Scooters remained popular. In Germany, BMW introduced

the new K series in 1983 which continued their innovative tradition by using a unique engine layout. Small machines were built by companies throughout Europe and the collapse of the Iron Curtain made motorcycles produced in the countries of Eastern Europe more familiar to purchasers in the West.

At the start of 1995 Europe had become the world leader in innovation and style. The Japanese manufacturers learned that introducing new models annually worked well in the boom years, but not during world recession. Their strategies included longer model runs and a return to serving the need for simple, basic transport – the reason they had initially become successful.

TRIUMPH 1992 TRIDENT
When Triumph closed in 1983 the name was bought by businessman John Bloor. In total secrecy he built a new factory and created a line of new and modern models, launched in 1990. Three-cylinder and four-cylinder machines were listed, but the 885cc triple engine proved the most popular.

USA: IT'S A HARLEY

HARLEY-DAVIDSON 1990 FAT BOY

The development of the American motorcycle industry began early in the 20th century. Some models were produced wholly in the United States, others used imported engines. Indian were founded in 1901, followed by Harley-Davidson in 1903; from modest beginnings both eventually expanded to dominate their market.

Many other firms built motorcycles for the American market during those early years, but these small concerns were unable to remain in business for long. American motorcycles had to be able to cope with vast distances on straight but poorly-surfaced roads outside the towns. These conditions called for robust motorcycles – any that lacked the necessary strength soon fell by the wayside. The machines that outlasted the others were stoutly constructed, resulting in an increase in the weight that required extra power to haul them along. So inevitably engines increased in size.

PENNINGTON 1897
An American who sold his patent rights for a reputed £100,000. This was one of the two machines built and had a directly-connected, twin-cylinder engine devoid of cooling fins. A needle valve in the inlet was both control and carburettor.

APACHE 1907
This Denver-built motorcycle was credited with using their own 36 cu. in. engine, but this is actually a Thor motor built by the Aurora Automatic Machinery Co of Illinois, near Chicago. Thor built their own machines and supplied a number of the early American firms including Indian.

APACHE 1907
The handlebar controls are linked to the rack-and-pinion, which are connected to the engine by rods and levers. Hand controls at the points of connection provide a back-up should the bar controls fail. The whole complex arrangement is shown in detail on this fine restoration.

SHAW 1908
This firm was based in Galesburg, Kansas, and made their own engines in two sizes. The engine situated on the downtube, the belt drive, and the jockey pulley to tension the drive are typical of the period. Braced forks and no suspension confirm this as a lightweight model.

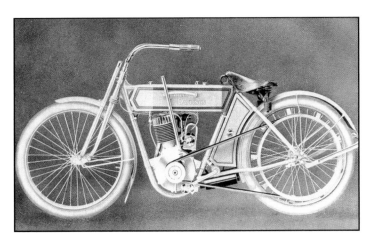

HARLEY-DAVIDSON 1911 MODEL 7A
Harley-Davidson began with a single-cylinder model in 1903 and continued to build these machines for a number of years. This model was fitted with an automatic inlet valve and optional magneto ignition. The company fitted mechanical inlet valves to these models in 1913.

HARLEY-DAVIDSON 1911 MODEL 7D
The first 1909 twin was not a success, so this model set the standard with the narrow, 45-degree angle between the cylinders. The twins had mechanically opened inlet valves from the start and a magneto ignition option was available.

PIERCE 1912
This firm was based in Buffalo, New York. Most of their machines had an in-line, four-cylinder engine. The frame was made from massive tubes that doubled as petrol and oil tanks. The Pierce was first seen in 1909, here with a Belgian FN and British Wilkinson four.

HARLEY-DAVIDSON 1913 MODEL 9
For 1913 there was a choice of belt or chain drive for the single-cylinder model, which continued the successful Harley-Davidson approach of fitting a lightly-stressed engine in strong cycle parts that suited the American roads of the time.

INDIAN 1913 TWIN
Pivoted-fork rear suspension and a kickstarter were two of the new features found on the 1913 61 cu. in. twin. The overhead inlet and side exhaust valves from the first models were retained. Indian twins continued to use a two-speed gearbox until 1915.

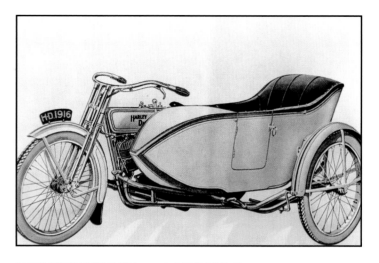

HARLEY-DAVIDSON 1916 MODEL 16C
This single was fitted with magneto ignition and a three-speed gearbox with chain drive to the rear wheel. The firm adopted leading-link front forks while the tank was given a rounded form in place of the older angular one.

HARLEY-DAVIDSON 1916 SIDECAR B
The firm listed several sidecars for most years of production. This is a typical example for the British and Japanese markets where people drive on the left. In those days both rider and passenger got wet when it rained.

INDIAN 1916 FEATHERWEIGHT
This was fashioned on British lines with a small, 13.5 cu. in. two-stroke engine, three-speed gearbox and all-chain drive. It had rocking forks for front suspension and a rigid frame, but proved unreliable so was only listed for one year. Now a rare model, this one was seen at Daytona in 1995.

INDIAN 1917 LIGHT TWIN
The engine unit of the light twin was smooth and quiet, but proved unpopular with buyers who were already seeking sports models rather than basic transport.

In order to obtain more capacity most firms simply added a second cylinder to their single, so that the majority of firms soon had a V-twin in the range. This engine type was to remain as the American standard down the years. However, for refinement some firms looked to the in-line, four-cylinder engine type with shaft drive, and in 1909 the Pierce Four joined the market. It was similar to the Belgian FN design in many ways, but had a superior engine and was distinguished by its frame, which was constructed in 9 cm/3.5 in. tubing that doubled as the petrol and oil tanks.

The majority of the market stayed with singles and V-twins, but before the year 1910 ended the Model T Ford had begun to cast its long shadow over the automotive industry. The real challenge came in 1915 when Ford was able to slash the prices of its cars following the introduction of the assembly line. This action changed the nature of private transport in America, but prior to the country's involvement in the First World War (1917-18), the motorcycle industry went through a boom period. More firms sprang up, most producing large-capacity V-twins. The need to economise on fuel was not a problem, thanks to the low price of petrol.

Large engines revealed the weakness of using a belt drive. American firms therefore turned to chain drive well in advance of the European competitors. The general riding conditions – long distances, over poor road surfaces – required well-sprung forks, saddles and footboards. Other features that appeared early on the American scene were three-speed gearboxes, drum rear brakes, full electric lighting and twistgrip throttles. Rear suspension was available from some firms, but was not common. The use of front brakes lagged well behind their introduction in Europe: American riders thought them unnecessary – even dangerous, with the potential to lock the front wheel on the poor road surfaces they encountered in country areas.

From as early as 1903 there were competitions and long distance rides, sometimes coast-to-coast. By 1910 the law restricted these races, but some remained into the modern era, from east to west or north to south, the latter for the Three Flags ride from Canada to Mexico.

During the early years the board tracks first appeared – steeply banked motordromes with a wooden surface and a circuit length from 550m/600 yds to over 1.6 km/1 mile. They were incredibly dangerous and spectacular; machines lapped in excess of 145 km/90 miles per hour. The riders raced shoulder-to-shoulder, and it was virtual-

READING-STANDARD 1917
Side-valve engines were brought to the United States by Reading-Standard, which produced them from 1903 to 1922. This is a typical example of their conventional but well-equipped V-twin machines, usually of 61 cu. in. capacity, with gearbox and leading-link forks.

ly inevitable that a major tragedy would occur. In 1912 it happened – two riders and six spectators died at Newark, New Jersey. The boards lingered on into the 1930s. Some were used for record attempts, laps at 190 km/120 miles per hour were feasible by the 1920s, but in time all the tracks fell or blew down, or were demolished.

American firms were able to take advantage of the conflict in Europe during the First World War. While their European competitors switched to making armaments, the Americans exported world-wide. When the United States entered the war in 1917, American motorcycle manufacturers then built for the services. After the war the

American industry was better placed than the European to resume civilian production. By contrast, the European economies were in shreds.

During the years after the war the American industry dwindled to just four makes. The public preferred the cheap and more sociable alternative of the car. Motorcycle firms were forced to rely for business on enthusiasts and law enforcement and other government agencies. However, motorcyclists in other countries were attracted by the robust reputation of the American motorcycles, and so provided useful export markets.

The 1920s were a period in which engines were refined.

Ventures in new directions were only made occasionally, and the main line of development continued to be the V-twins, although some bikes used singles and in-line fours. Competition helped to advance technology, which was suited to the American racing scene of tracks ranging from the motordromes to dirt, and included paved circuits and the ovals.

The Wall Street Crash of October 1929 marked the beginning of the Depression. Only two manufacturers, Harley-Davidson and Indian, survived into the 1930s. Police and other service machines continued to supply their main source of business. The collapse in sales led to cutbacks on racing teams which were now seen as a luxury. It did not help that fewer people had money to spend, and spectators had learned there was a big difference between the machines they saw raced and the ones they actually rode.

The solution was Class C racing, which used stock production machines with some modifications. The rules were designed to suit the 45 cu. in. V-twins built by the two remaining firms, although imports were occasionally raced with them. There were also events with larger and faster machines but, in the main, Class C became the most popular event, because mechanics learned how to make the motorcycles very fast and the number of entrants increased as more people could afford to take part.

This situation revived American racing and helped the industry to survive through the lean years of the 1930s. In the main they continued to use V-twin engines which had served them well for so long and would continue to do so. The manufacturers kept producing tough machines, although paved highways now stretched through most of the United States. Customers were used to them, and they remained popular in export markets.

America's participation in the Second World War (1941-45) brought real changes. The factories produced machines for the armed forces while thousands of American men and women had the chance to ride European motorcycles in the terrain for which they were designed. Most were British, German and Italian wartime models but there was a good sprinkling of others. The Americans discovered that there was an alternative to the tough, heavy V-twin.

The light models from Europe had better road-holding

INDIAN 1917 LIGHT TWIN
Indian replaced their unsuccessful two-stroke with this model. It had a 15.68 cu. in. flat-twin, side-valve engine, three-speed gearbox and all-chain drive. It kept the rocking fork from the two-stroke, but changed to the usual Indian leaf-spring, trailing-link design for 1918.

HARLEY-DAVIDSON 1916 MODEL 16F
By this time the engine was rated as 7-9hp and the whole machine looked much more complete, but it still lacked a front brake. The rear was the internal-expanding drum type that used a band rather than shoes inside the drum.

HARLEY-DAVIDSON 1923 MODEL 23J
The basic Harley-Davidson V-twin with overhead inlet valve and side exhaust reached this form for the 1920s. There were continual improvements over the years, but the basic concept of a high power-to-weight ratio combined with tough parts, continued to offer a reliable machine that was easy to ride over long distances.

abilities and good brakes and acceleration, qualities suited to the sinuous roads found there. American riders, once back home, wanted more of the same; European manufacturers, especially British ones, were keen to create a new export market. So began the American love affair with British machines, predominately Triumph and BSA twins, but including most other types.

Indian and Harley-Davidson fought back, but Indian was in decline and its production of V-twins had ceased by 1953. A vertical twin was added to the range to compete against the imports, but these machines were too unreliable to achieve any real success. Later the Indian name was linked to a variety of other models but none made an impact on the American market.

Harley-Davidson continued to develop the V-twin in various formats. They came large or small, with side valves or overhead valves (ohv). In time the side-valve solos were dropped, although the Servi-Car, a motorcycle with twin rear wheels and a rear box between them popular with the police, continued in production into the 1970s.

As the years went by the overhead valve V-twins gained telescopic front forks, rear suspension and electric start, while unit construction of the engine and gearbox appeared on one model in the 1950s. This was to develop alongside the existing range so that even today Harley-Davidsons may have the engine separate from or built with the gearbox.

Aside from their main V-twin line, Harley entered the small-capacity market after the war. For this they adopted the same prewar German DKW design used by the BSA Bantam, Russian Voskhod and Yamaha Red Dragonfly. The result was their first two-stroke engine, of 125cc capacity, which was in the range for over a decade. During that time it gained telescopic front forks and was joined by a 165cc version, both known as the Hummer. In the 1960s these were replaced by a series of similar models carrying names such as Super 10, Ranger, Scat, Pacer and Bobcat. There was a scooter, the Topper, which used the 165cc engine, but had automatic transmission. It arrived in 1959, too late for the scooter boom, so production was stopped after a few years.

By the 1960s, Harley were on another tack, making

NER-A-CAR 1923
A machine that used a variety of engines and a friction drive as a means of altering the gears. The low build and hub-centre steering gave it excellent road holding and good stability while the ample front mudguard was very effective in bad weather. It was built in Britain under licence where a four-stroke engine and conventional gearbox were used.

HARLEY-DAVIDSON 1924 MODEL JD
This two-seat sidecar, with twin screens to protect the front and rear passengers under the hood, is hitched to a 12hp 74 cu. in. motorcycle. The rear section could be folded shut to provide luggage space when only the front seat was occupied.

HENDERSON 1925 MODEL K
This firm built four-cylinder models from its launch in 1912 and the design continued after its sale to Excelsior in 1918. This model introduced a sloping tank, but the in-line engine and chain final drive remained. At this time the capacity was 80 cu in, and the top speed was 128 km/80 miles per hour.

small machines in collaboration with Aermacchi in Italy, in whom they had a 50 per cent stake. The first model to be produced as a result was the 250cc Sprint, a fine example of an Italian motorcycle but not really suited to the American market. Later came the 350cc Sprint, Leggero mopeds and small two-strokes.

In 1969, Harley-Davidson were bought by American Machine Foundry (AMF), and in 1973 the Italian models were changed to a new line of two-strokes that proved mediocre when compared with the Japanese models. Then, in 1978, AMF sold Aermacchi to Cagiva which brought the Italian connection to an end.

During this period the V-twin ranges had settled into two forms, the Electra Glide as the ultimate tourer, and the unit construction Sportster. Both had a variety of specifications, enhanced by a massive catalogue of options and extras for the machine and equipment for the rider.

Harley-Davidson dominated American sports motorcycling from the 1950s to the 1960s, racing their side-valve machines. The factory remained successful thanks to their in-depth knowledge of the engine type and a galaxy of fast, determined riders. This changed in the 1970s with the advent of the big Japanese two-stroke racers in some events, but overall Harley was at the forefront of the US

domestic scene. In Europe their Aermacchi arm had real success in world championship races, taking several world titles from 1974 to 1976; but competition racing was really divorced from the traditional Harley machines.

At the beginning of the 1970s, Harley introduced a new motorcycle combining features from the two existing ranges. From this a complete new range was developed and expanded during the decade. In 1981, AMF sold Harley to a group that included the founding families, employees and AMF people.

Within a year a further new range was available to take the firm into the 1990s. The V-twin format remained and it gained a customer loyalty unprecedented for any other firm or product, the envy of firms world-wide.

Harley-Davidson has been the American industry for some 40 years. During that time there have been other makes built in the United States, but on a small, local scale, usually producing machines of less capacity. The same applied to Canada, Mexico and South America. However, the major Japanese firms have set up plants in South America and the United States.

Thus, while Harley-Davidson rides high, the other major motorcycle manufacturers in the United States are Honda and Kawasaki.

HARLEY-DAVIDSON 1928 MX PARCELCAR This commercial sidecar, designed to transport goods and equipment for business, was listed by the firm for many years. This one is attached to a 61 cu. in. twin.

HARLEY-DAVIDSON 1928 21 OHV
The firm offered these single-cylinder machines in side-valve and overhead-valve formats. The side-valve ones sold better than the ohv versions. The front brake, which had previously been considered unnecessary on account of the unpaved roads then common in the United States, was introduced for the 1928 models, when paved roads were becoming commonplace.

HARLEY-DAVIDSON 1928 21 SV
This is the side-valve version of the single that was built in a 30 cu. in. size for 1930. Easy to ride and service, the model suited the buyer who was not yet experienced enough to ride a large twin.

HARLEY-DAVIDSON 1928 74
Nearing the end of production, the original V-twin with overhead inlet and side exhaust valves was developed to this form. It was soon to be replaced by new models, some with side valves, others with overhead.

INDIAN 1928 SCOUT
For many years Indian produced the 37 cu. in. Scout along with the much larger 61 cu. in. Chief for use with sidecars. Both had V-twin, side-valve engines with a three-speed gearbox bolted to the crankcase and driven by a helical-gear primary drive working inside a cast-aluminium case. These modern, noisy gears were able to outlast the rest of the machine.

HARLEY-DAVIDSON 1930 45
During 1928 the firm launched the first of their side-valve twins, the 45 or model D. The 45 cu. in. engine was basic and robust, essential attributes during the Depression. Versions with larger engines were also available.

HARLEY-DAVIDSON 1930 SPORTS SIDECAR
The classic bullet shape of sidecar bodies used in the United States and Europe has acquired modern lines in this example. The motorcycle in this case is the 45, with its powerful V-twin.

HARLEY-DAVIDSON 1930 74
This machine had a new 74 cu. in. engine with side valves to replace the older type from 1911. It was powerful and had massive torque for heavy loads. There were two sizes that remained in production into the postwar period.

HARLEY-DAVIDSON 1930 PACKAGE TRUCK
This version of sidecar was coupled with the side-valve models and were used for many years. These outfits benefited from their low fuel consumption and the ability to get through heavy traffic.

HARLEY-DAVIDSON 1934 74
Massive V-twin and sports sidecar with a spare wheel in the style of the mid-1930s. This was a difficult sales period, when every endeavour was made to bring buyers into the showroom and persuade them to purchase.

HENDERSON 1931
This was the last year of production for the Henderson firm that began building fours in 1912. Initially, the passenger was perched over the fuel tank in front of the rider, later they reverted to the more normal position. This model KJ has a 80 cu. in. engine with overhead inlet valves and a five-bearing crankshaft.

HARLEY-DAVIDSON 1934 74
This is a restored V-twin with a 74 cu. in. engine, photographed in 1993 in the United Kingdom.

HARLEY-DAVIDSON 1934 74
A solo machine with a fine side-valve engine that powered it down the highway. This model still had leading-link front forks; but there were drum brakes for both wheels and full electric equipment.

HARLEY-DAVIDSON 1934 30-50 SV
Built in 21 cu. in. and 30.5 cu. in. formats, these singles continued to offer basic and reliable transport at a time when the cost of a V-twin was beyond many people.

INDIAN 1940 FOUR
Indian moved to four cylinders by buying the Ace design with the overhead inlet and side exhaust valves. This layout was reversed between 1936 and 1937, but changed back in 1938 when the engine had the cylinders cast in pairs to produce a pleasing line. The skirted fenders were adopted for the 1940 models with plunger rear suspension.

HARLEY-DAVIDSON 1934 45
The 45 cu. in. V-twin had a rear fender unique to that year, but it was the last for the toolbox mounted on the front forks. Thus, Harleys changed from year to year in many small ways, yet retained the concept set many years ago of using a strong engine in a strong chassis.

HARLEY-DAVIDSON 1937 SERVI-CAR
This model was based on the 45 and was designed to collect cars. It was connected by tow bar to the car which hauled it back to the garage. It was popular with police departments for removing vechicles from unwanted locations, and could still to be seen in the United States in the 1990s.

HARLEY-DAVIDSON 1937 KNUCKLEHEAD
Harley-Davidson launched the model E in 1936. It was a 61 cu. in. ohv that became known as the Knucklehead as a result of the shape of its rocker box. The forerunner of the modern line, it had an overhead-valve engine, four speeds and dry-sump lubrication – along with a fresh new style.

INDIAN 1940 FOUR
The engine unit of the Indian Four in its final form adopted from 1938 had fine lines and the valve gear was fully enclosed and lubricated, unlike the older engines, which had exposed pushrods that allowed the dirt in and the oil out.

HARLEY-DAVIDSON 1942 KNUCKLEHEAD
The frame, tank and wheels of the 1937 motorcycle were used for the 74 cu. in. and 80 cu. in. models. In 1941, the larger 74 ohv was introduced and was produced into the postwar period. This is a restored machine, seen at a late-1994 show.

SIMPLEX 1941 SERVI-CYCLE
The countershaft behind the 7.5 cu. in. two-stroke engine and transmission acted as a clutch by loosening the belt tension when operated. Later it also served to adjust the pulley ratios.

HARLEY-DAVIDSON 1937 80
First seen in 1935, this model had a massive 80 cu. in. engine in the stock cycle parts. It offered huge torque while retaining the usual Harley qualities of reliability, easy servicing and good spares backup.

INDIAN 1940 MODEL 741
Designed to be sold to the services, this model had a 30 cu. in. engine derived from the older Scout Pony of the 1930s. Most went to the Allied forces in Europe and the Far East rather than the United States, so they are now more common outside America.

SIMPLEX 1941 SERVI-CYCLE
This American curio, built in New Orleans from the late 1930s to the 1960s, used an industrial engine and belt drive.

HARLEY-DAVIDSON 1942 WLA
Harley-Davidson built this modified 45 for the armed services during the war. Many were kept in Europe after the war.

INDIAN 1941 841
This model, built to service specifications, had a transverse-mounted 45 cu. in. V-twin to drive a four-speed gearbox with power transmitted by shaft to the rear wheel. Front forks were girders with a telescopic look to them while plungers served the rear wheel. About a thousand were built, few were used in service, but some of the design details were used in the postwar period.

INDIAN 1944 741
The stock service model with full complement of bags and a machine gun in the special holder. This one was restored in 1982 in a typical army finish and markings. The service specification required modest performance and complete reliability.

INDIAN 1946 CHIEF
In 1934, the gear primary drive was replaced by a chain, but this remained in an oil bath case, so continued to outlast the machine while eliminating the gear whine of the past. Immediately after the war, the Chief was the only Indian motorcycle in production. The firm continued with the skirted fenders, but adopted the telescopic-style girder forks from the 841 model and softer rear suspension. This finely restored example was seen at Daytona in 1995.

HARLEY-DAVIDSON 1947 KNUCKLEHEAD
This was the last year for the original style of ohv Knucklehead, because the Panhead model was introduced in 1948. It had light-alloy cylinder heads, hydraulic valve lifters and a new style of rocker box cover which gave rise to the new name.

HARLEY-DAVIDSON 1947 125
This small two-stroke was a complete change for the firm. It was a copy of the German DKW that was also built by BSA, Yamaha, IFA and Voskhod. The125cc had unit construction, three speeds and a reputation for reliability.

HARLEY-DAVIDSON 1947 45
This motorcycle was seen at Brands Hatch in 1994. Although replaced in 1952 as a solo, it continued in Servi-Car form for many more years. This example is a Dutch outfit, hence the sidecar on the right.

INDIAN 1947 CHIEF
There were few changes for the 1947 model, the massive Chief continued with side-valve, V-twin power, stylish and skirted fenders and a number of detail alterations.

and highways and are making them safe for travel. And in commercial use, alert business men are finding Harley-Davidsons indispensable in handling service calls and light deliveries with speed, dispatch and great economy.

45 TWIN

HARLEY-DAVIDSON 1948 45
The 45 kept the leading-link front forks used since its introduction. Little else had altered over the two decades of production other than the annual styling and cosmetic changes.

INDIAN 1950 CHIEF
For its final years the Chief's engine was increased to 80 cu. in., and this was reflected in the tank badges. The gear lever visible in the foreground was connected to either a three-speed or four-speed gearbox.

HARLEY-DAVIDSON 1948 PANHEAD 61
The Panhead was produced with hydraulic valve lifters, new light-alloy cylinder heads and rocker box covers (shown here) shaped like baking trays, hence the nickname. This was the only year the model combined these features with the leading-link front forks.

HARLEY-DAVIDSON 1948 PANHEAD 74
The left side of the overhead-valve V-twin is shown here. These models were essentially the same apart from the engine capacity. The smaller ones were dropped after 1952, but the larger stayed in production up to 1980.

INDIAN 1949 SCOUT
Indian decided to offer singles and vertical twins in the British style in 1949. The singles were soon dropped and the 440cc Scout (shown here) was increased to 500cc in 1950, but they had a reputation for technical problems and poor assembly.

HARLEY-DAVIDSON 1949 HYDRA-GLIDE
For 1949 the big V-twins changed to telescopic front forks and were called Hydra-Glides, regardless of the engine capacity. They were built in this form up to 1957, after which the remaining 74 in the product range was given rear suspension and became the Duo-Glide.

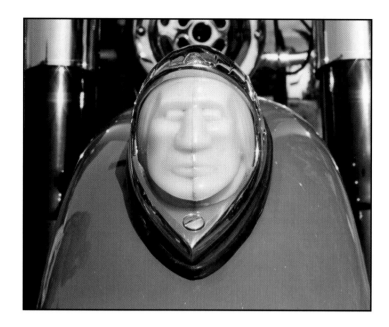

INDIAN 1950 CHIEF
This front mudguard detail was used by Indian on Chief models with skirted fenders.

INDIAN 1951 WARRIOR
The Scout became the Warrior for 1950 when engine capacity was increased to 30 cu. in. and some parts were changed to eradicate problems. But cheap components continued to cause trouble when starting the motorcycle.

HARLEY-DAVIDSON 1951 HUMMER
This model became the Tele-Glide when the telescopic front forks were added, later joined by a 10 cu. in. model, when both were known as the Hummer. They were manufactured until 1959, but enthusiasts never accepted them as true Harley-Davidsons.

INDIAN 1952 CHIEF
Deviations from the stock model are common with American motorcycles, as a result of owners changing parts for others more to their liking. In this example of the final form of the Chief, a fork cowling and one fitted to the engine side between the exhaust pipes (missing from this example) were added.

INDIAN 1953 CHIEF
The Chief and other Indian motorcycles went out of production in 1953, although the name was to continue. Reproduction parts for these models are still easy to find.

HARLEY-DAVIDSON 1954 KH
The K series introduced unit construction, footchange and front and rear suspension to Harley-Davidson, but kept the side valves of the old 45 and the same capacity. Initially lacking power, the engine was enlarged to 55 cu. in. in 1954 and in 1957 overhead valves were added and the motorcyle became the Sportster.

HARLEY-DAVIDSON 1954 HYDRA-GLIDE
A typical example of the large Harleys during the 1950s before rear suspension was introduced in 1958. Up to then the front forks, fat-section tyres and a massive buddy seat spring-mounted into the frame cushioned the riders from road shocks; this combination worked well.

INDIAN 1957 HOUNDS ARROW
This model was a Royal Enfield 15 cu. in. Clipper modified for trail riding, but it retained the separate engine and gearbox. Listed as the Fire Arrow in road form, both models were later based on the unit-construction 15 cu. in. Crusader model.

HARLEY-DAVIDSON 1966 KR
The unit-construction model K with 45 cu. in. side-valve engine was raced by the factory and private owners for many years. It was very successful up to 1969 on American flat-track ovals, hill climbs and on the road-and-beach circuit at Daytona. The model shown here was at Daytona in 1995, typical of the type, but most varied in detail.

LLOYD PAKTRAK
Very basic models that had a stationary engine for power. They were built and used in cities and towns across the United States in the postwar period. This example has a rear track instead of a simple wheel. Most were used for short-distance transport.

INDIAN 1955 TRAILBLAZER
In 1955 four of British Royal Enfield models, with slight alterations, went on sale in the United States bearing the Indian badge. This one is a 42 cu. in. Meteor fitted with a crankshaft-mounted alternator, a feature that did not appear until 1956 in the United Kingdom.

HARLEY-DAVIDSON 1969 XR-750
For years American racing rules limited ohv machines to 500cc, but allowed side-valve models to have 750cc engines. When the rules were changed in 1969, Harley-Davidson introduced this ohv XR-750. At first it had this fragile iron engine, but the alloy one of 1972 was a winner for two decades.

HARLEY-DAVIDSON 1975 X90
Harley-Davidson took a 50 per cent stake in the Italian firm
Aermacchi from 1960 to 1978. Harley imported many
Aermacchi machines including a series of two-strokes, one
of which is shown here. It is a 90cc off-road model for the
young, sold alongside other models up to 250cc.

COOPER 1972 250
Conceived in the United States, but built at Saltillo in
northern Mexico, this machine used a two-stroke engine
with a five-speed gearbox in a frame suspended on
Betor forks and Boge rear dampers. This gave the machine
good balance and handling. It was tested in the Mexican
desert and the Californian mountains.

INDIAN 1976 MI-175
The Indian name was revived in 1970 to offer a range of
machines including some small off-road models powered by
two-stroke engines. These were imported to Europe in 1976, but
failed to make much of an impression on the market.

ROKON 1976 TRAILBREAKER
This is an unusual model built in Keene, New Hampshire, and powered by a 8 cu. in. Chrysler two-stroke engine. It featured these enormous wheels, both of which were driven. There were three speeds, automatic clutch, front disc brakes and it was able to climb slopes at an incredible angle.

HARLEY-DAVIDSON 1975 SUPER GLIDE
In 1971 Harley created a new line of V-twins by taking the existing Glide model and fitting the Sportster forks and front wheel. It proved a popular combination and led to the introduction of an extensive range of models. Back in 1966, the engine had a new rocker box and hence a new name, 'Shovelhead'.

HARLEY-DAVIDSON 1982 TOUR GLIDE CLASSIC
The Glide series offered the Harley buyer the ultimate in equipment. Development forward brought the range from the Duo-Glide to the Electra Glide, when an electric starter was added in 1965. There were several versions, but all were based on the idea of long-distance touring.

CAN-AM 1979 MX-5
These advanced machines, built by Bombardier in Canada, were the product of the experience and ability of ex-BSA World Champion Jeff Smith. This model was listed in 248cc and 366cc sizes and was fully up to date for its time. The firm concentrated on building snowmobiles and boats in later years.

HARLEY-DAVIDSON 1986 SUPER GLIDE
This was the entry-level model among the big twins at that time. Its seat height was actually lower than that of the Low Rider of the same year. It continued the Harley style of mixing parts to provide variety and an array of models.

HARLEY-DAVIDSON 1986 SOFTAIL CUSTOM
This model combined the hidden rear suspension of the Softail with the solid rear wheel of the Disc Glide and the seat, bars and other features of the custom models. It became a popular model in an extensive line, most of which had revised engines installed in 1984.

73

HARLEY-DAVIDSON 1987 HERITAGE SOFTAIL
This model added the style and finish of the past to the
Softail line and proved popular with riders. Hiding the rear
suspension units was not a new feature, but the firm managed to impart their own signature to it.

HARLEY-DAVIDSON 1990 ELECTRA GLIDE
ULTRA CLASSIC
This model continued the Harley-Davidson concept of having the ultimate in equipment. It came with top box, panniers, extra lights, CB radio, full sound system, fairing and special paint. It was a large and heavy machine, but it could transport two people and all their luggage anywhere.

HARLEY-DAVIDSON 1988 SPRINGER SOFTAIL
With this Super Glide model the company fitted a modernised version of the old leading-link front forks along with Softail rear suspension, to produce the look of their early machines; this is a model from 1992.

HARLEY-DAVIDSON 1990 FAT BOY
This new style from Harley-Davidson, in the Super Glide series, had solid wheels and a grey paint job for panels and frame to give it an all-in-one appearance. It was popular with customers and stayed in the range.

**HARLEY-DAVIDSON 1995 ELECTRA GLIDE
ULTRA CLASSIC**
This is the 30th anniversary edition of the Electra Glide
model first seen in 1965 and equipped and finished to suit.
The firm often produced special versions of their stock
models for such occasions to help sales along.

HARLEY-DAVIDSON 1995 SPORTSTER
The unit-construction engine powered the Sportster line
from its inception in 1957 until 1986 when the engine had a
major revamp.

SPECIAL 1995
This innovative motorcycle was seen at Daytona in 1995. It is powered by a Honda Gold Wing engine, has a reverse gear and an outrigger wheel on each side. Thus, it is as wide as a truck.

HARLEY-DAVIDSON 1995 DYNA SUPER GLIDE
This series kept the twin rear shocks on view, instead of using the Softail concept to hide them. It was produced in various custom styles that were all related.

HARLEY-DAVIDSON 1995
A customised motorcycle shown by the firm at Daytona in 1995
had a tank bearing the words 'Biker Blues', and was finished in
a blue denim colour on the frame, forks, fenders and other parts.
Many Harley-Davidson motorcycles have been customised by
their owners in the same way as this example.

BRITAIN: CLASSICAL TO RETRO

TRIUMPH 1971 TRIDENT

The British motorcycle industry began against a background of restrictive legislation that held back pioneering efforts for several years. Until legislation was changed in 1896, powered vehicle speeds were restricted to 6.4 km/4 miles per hour. However, once the manufacturers were freed from such limitations, they were able to take advantage of the advances already made in Europe. Engine parts were imported from France and Belgium because there were no suppliers in Britain, but there were many skilled cycle mechanics and designers.

Around the turn of the century many small British bicycle-making firms ventured into the motorcycle trade by taking an imported engine and bolting it to a heavy-duty frame. Then, by applying a nice transfer on the headstock, another model was launched. Many of these firms were retailers who saw the newfangled powered machine as a means of improving their business, both through the sale of a more expensive product and the need for much

EXCELSIOR 1902
Typical early machine with the engine hung from the down-tube and controlled by a row of taps mounted to the petrol tank. Rigid forks made for a hard ride on the narrow-section tyres and a bicycle front brake did little for stopping.

WEARWELL 1903
Some tricycles had the two wheels at the front – often a simple addition to an existing solo model – producing the forecar, where the passenger could find themselves nearest to the accident!

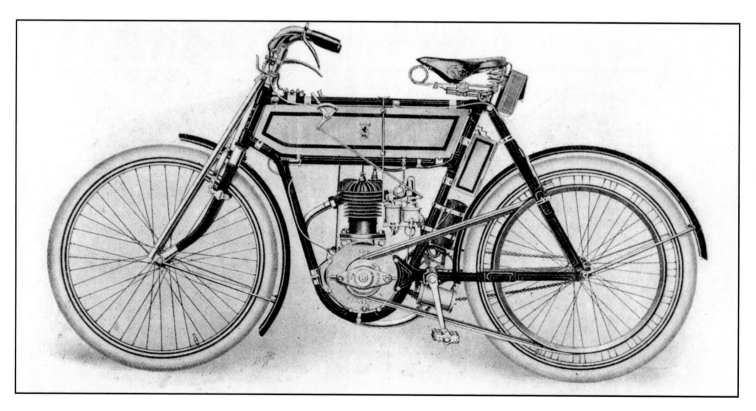

CLARENDON 1904
This typical advertisement from the early 1900s shows the engine position adopted by the Werner brothers and taken up by virtually every manufacturer. The essence of the design was that the pedals made way for the gearbox.

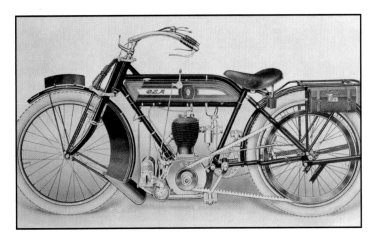

BSA 1913
BSA came late to the powered transport business. Their first machine, similar to this example, was built in 1910. BSA offered good quality, reliability, spares and service.

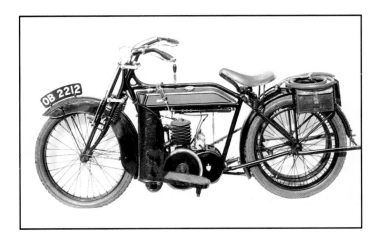

JAMES 1914
This 225cc two-stroke, fitted with a two-speed gearbox and chain-and-belt transmission, has unusual cylinder finning, a distinguishing feature of James' machines of the period.

CAMPION 1916
Ambulance sidecar outfits such as these were a feature at home and in the front line during the Great War, often able to bring back casualties from locations impossible for a truck to reach. The side-valve, V-twin engines were especially suited to this type of work.

NORTON 1920s
The side-valve Norton of the flat-tank era was one of the most desirable machines. Offered in two sizes and to various specifications, it was fast and reliable although the front brake was not going to stop it quickly. The basic engine and its 79 x 100 mm/3 x 4 in. dimensions plus 490cc capacity, was listed by the firm for over half a century.

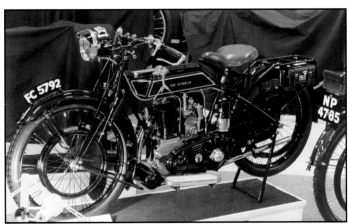

SUNBEAM 1923
This firm was renowned for the excellence of the black-and-gold finish of their machines. In 1923 they built side-valve singles in 347cc, 499cc and 599cc capacities, these being joined by overhead valve models during the following year. All were of high quality and enjoyed a fine reputation.

VELOCETTE 1930 KTT
Introduced in 1929, and based on a TT-winning design, the KTT was a mainstay of racing for years. Its fast, powerful 348cc ohc engine was used in models from Mk I to Mk VIII, by when it had deeper finning, rear suspension and still won TTs. From it was developed the similar KSS road model.

VINCENT-HRD 1929
Philip Vincent bought the rights to the HRD name in 1928 to carry out his ideas on frame and suspension design. Thus was born a famous marque. This model had a JAP side-valve engine, 500cc or 600cc, and a silencer attached to a moving fork member instead of the saddle support.

During the 1920s there were more motorcycles than cars on the roads and this dealer's large stock shows some of what was available. All sorts and sizes can be seen in this array of second-hand machines with a few sidecars in the background.

TRIUMPH 1930 CN
Britain's longest-running motorcycle manufacturer, Triumph's range of models in 1930 included a couple of side-valve singles like this example used by an AA patrolman. The 498cc CN and 549cc CSD were similar and offered reliable basic transport.

ROYAL ENFIELD 1939 RE
The RE was built for a Dutch firm that had lost its German DKW concession. It was a copy of the DKW enlarged from 98cc to 125cc. Produced from 1939 up to the 1960s, it was used by the British during the war and known as the 'Flying Flea', because it was often dropped by parachute.

after-sale service, even if their own expertise was little better than that of the customer.

Larger bicycle manufacturers delayed entering this industry. Norton and Triumph appeared as early as 1902, but BSA held off building their first motorcycle until 1910. All three companies became major motorcycle manufacturers.

By the end of 1910 machines had been developed to be strong and reliable. Most were without a clutch, were single–geared and belt-driven, yet they suited the needs of most owners at that time.

Alongside the many single-cylinder motorcycles, there was an array of V-twins and sidecar models which replaced the forecar and trailer of the past. The first TT

races in 1907 and the appearance of motorcycles at Brooklands a year after the track was opened, forced motorcycle technology forward, but the transmission systems lagged behind.

It was the move of the TT to the Mountain course in 1911, plus the success of the American Indian two-speed machines when they took the first three places in the Senior race, that started the trend towards gears. It took time, but the countershaft gearbox and all-chain drive gradually became universal, although belt drive was used into the 1920s. There were always one or two firms that opted to produce shaft-drive models.

Most of these developments took place a few years before the First World War. Production models were used

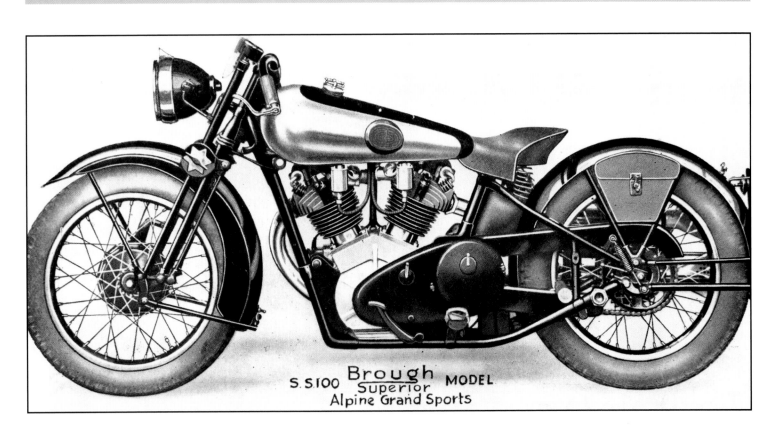

BROUGH-SUPERIOR 1934 SS100
George Brough built the kind of machines he liked to ride – expensive, fast and exciting. This Alpine Grand Sports model was fitted with a 995cc JAP engine and was typical of the type.

SCOTT 1934 FLYING SQUIRREL
An advanced machine in 1910, with twin-cylinders, a watercooled two-stroke engine and angular tank.

BSA 1935 MODEL G
A large-capacity V-twin was part of BSA's line from 1920 to 1940. Used mainly with a sidecar, it had the ability to cope with the largest of loads. BSA's usual reliability and wide availability of spares, made it a popular choice.

OEC 1938 COMMANDER
The Osborn Engineering Company built machines of differing sizes using engines from Villiers, Blackburne, Sturmey-Archer, JAP, Matchless and AJS. Famous for the curious front fork design (shown here) offered as far back as 1927, in this case fitted to a model using an AJS engine.

by the armed forces during the war, then the government contracted some manufacturers to produce specific models from their existing ranges for the military to use, while other companies were directed to produce other materials for the war effort.

The British dispatch rider commonly had the use of a trusty Triumph, usually the model H, a typical single-cylinder machine which had a three-speed gearbox and a belt for the final drive. The main alternative was the Douglas flat-twin which had two speeds and belt final drive. BSA, Ariel, P&M and Rudge singles were also used, but to a lesser degree. Clyno V-twin sidecars and Scott two-stroke twins were used as ambulances.

After the war there was a boom period, but demand far exceeded supply as industry struggled to return to peace-time production. Technical developments on air-cooled engines achieved during wartime led to the use of better materials, lubricants and designs on chain-driven singles and twins, with a countershaft gearbox, plus small two-strokes with limited use of belt drive. By the end of the decade British motorcycles had adopted the saddle tank style.

There was a small-scale scooter boom at the beginning of the 1920s, but it was not on anything like the scale that would occur some 30 years later. But hard times were to come. The Depression was a major factor in this period, but manufacturers' woes were exacerbated by the trend towards the car. Soon there were more of them on the road than motorcycles. Some firms tried to compete by slashing prices, but more switched to other products.

Despite this poor industrial climate, manufacturers continued to develop the technology. Both Ariel and Matchless exhibited overhead-camshaft fours at the 1930 motorcycle show. These remained in production for some years, the Ariel continuing in a ohv form. British machines continued their tradition of success on the race circuits, although they lost their hold on the 250cc and then the 500cc classes to German and Italian models .

Then came the Second World War, and once again firms either converted to weapons-making or filled their paint guns with khaki and sprayed military colours over a small selection of their model range for use by the services. Most were side-valve singles from BSA and Norton, but ohv models were supplied by Ariel, Royal Enfield and Triumph, small two-strokes came from James, Enfield and Welbike, and Matchless offered its model with telescopic forks. Initially, the services commandeered civilian machines and any stocks at the maker's works, but this array of diverse models proved hard to service, so they were soon replaced by standard issue machines.

NORTON 1938 ES2
The 490cc engine in overhead-valve form was still going strong in the late-1930s, offering good performance, reliability and easy maintenance. This one has had the mudguards changed but is otherwise original.

RUDGE 1939 ULSTER
A famous bicycle firm that began producing motorcycles in 1910 and soon built up a good reputation in competition and on the road. The Ulster had a four-valve head and was built throughout the 1930s as the top-of-the-range sports model.

There were tons of surplus motorcycles and spares at the end of the war, most sold off in lots to dealers. They were resprayed in black or sometimes maroon. The large amount of spares available ensured the machines could be kept on the road. Some spares, such as the electrics and carburettors, could be used to revitalise older machines.

At the end of the war Britain was heavily in debt and exports were the best way to pay it off. This put a curb on new ideas and designs, the urgent need for production calling for proven models in civilian finish. Most were essentially 1939 models with the addition of telescopic forks.

However, there were some innovative new designs from Douglas, Vincent, Sunbeam and Velocette. Others, such as the Wooler, were too advanced for the market, so only prototypes were built.

The postwar period saw the production of a number of clip-on engines for bicycles, and the concept worked well over short distances and across modest hills. Many of these were used as transport to work or to the station for the train into town.

During the late 1940s new machines remained a rare sight on British roads, most motorcyclists made do with prewar or ex-service models. Petrol rationing continued up to 1950 along with other shortages, so motorcycling for pleasure was limited to local runs. Most new models were vertical twins, following the lead of the prewar Triumph Speed Twin; by the end of the decade most major manufacturers had similar models.

Most small capacity models used Villiers two-stroke engines, but there were exceptions, such as the BSA Bantam and the Royal Enfield RE model, both 125cc. BSA developed the Bantam over the years as one of the company's most successful models. The RE had been launched in Holland in 1939. It proved to be a reliable motorcycle during the war and remained in the range into the 1960s.

There were few small four-strokes below 250cc, but the 150cc Triumph Terrier, later stretched into the 200cc Cub, was one while the LE Velocette had a water-cooled 150cc, flat-twin engine with side valves, that was also enlarged to 200cc. The Velocette had many other special features such as hand starting and gear change, shaft drive and built-in weather protection. It and the Triumph were to have long lives, well into the 1960s.

Sidecars continued to be popular, even though the driver was cut off from the passengers, a disadvantage compared with the more sociable interior of a car. As the prewar V-twins were no longer built, most owners used a 600cc side-valve single unless one of the new vertical twins could be bought. The massive 600cc ohv Panther was a good alternative, but the only V-twin available was the Vincent-HRD, which was essentially a high-speed and expensive sports model, far beyond most peoples' budget.

On the road-racing scene, British machines continued to win the 350cc, 500cc and sidecar classes, but new Italian designs indicated the trend. Italian manufacturers already had a grip on the smaller classes in which their British

**ARIEL
1939 SQUARE FOUR**
Ariel launched their first 498cc, overhead-camshaft four in 1931 during the Depression. It was developed into a 601cc, superseded in 1937 by the 997cc (shown here), which used simple overhead valves. It was smooth, fast and became known as the Squariel, a popular touring model that stayed in production for over two decades.

BSA 1940-45 M20
During the Second World War BSA concentrated on the side-valve M20 model, building over 126,000 of them. The design came from 1937 and ran on into the 1960s in a larger M21 form. Very basic but also very tough and spares are still available.

rivals no longer competed, and they looked set to capture larger ones when the world championships began in 1949.

However, Velocette captured the 350cc title in the first two years and AJS the 500cc in 1949. Then, in 1950, Norton produced the Featherbed version of their works model and recruited Geoff Duke to ride it. He was a sensation and only tyre failures at two of the classics prevented him taking his first 500cc title.

In 1951 Duke took both the 350cc and 500cc titles and retained the 350cc in 1952, but even his talent could no longer hold the Italian motorcycles at bay in the 500cc class. A bad crash did not help and he then left Norton whose machines continued to take the sidecar title up to 1953. This was essentially by courtesy of Eric Oliver, but in 1954 BMW started a 20-year domination of the class. Since those days there have been no world titles and few TT wins for British machines.

British road machines progressed slowly in the 1950s. Paint finishes became brighter, rear suspension became standardised and details changed, but all too often next year's models hardly differed from last year's. There was little attempt to produce innovative small machines, move

on from clip-on units to mopeds or to pick up on the scooter boom from Italy.

One spark of real innovation was the Ariel Leader launched in 1958. This was a truly fresh design that sought to offer the weather protection of the scooter with the performance and handling of the motorcycle. In addition, the machine was designed for mass production using steel pressings, alloy die-castings and plastic mouldings as far as was possible.

However, managers declined to make the investments that would have helped the British industry match competition from foriegn rivals. Despite the lack of new designs, the decade was a prosperous one for the industry. The best year was 1959. A large amount of this business came from handling imports. It was to prove a bad mistake.

Enclosure of the engine and gearbox had become a theme of the late 1950s but faded in the next decade to be replaced by the café-racer style, emphasised by the Triton. This combined the excellent Norton Featherbed frame and forks with the easily-tuned Triumph twin engine.

Firms offered more and more sporting machines while gradually turning their back on small models and ignoring the moped and scooter markets. The Japanese firms took a large share of this while British manufacturers concentrated on exporting large-capacity twins, the majority of which went to the United States. This reliance on a single market for almost all their sales was very dangerous.

There were machine updates in this effort, but in most cases the results continued to betray their old origins. Then the Japanese moved into the large-capacity market in Britain and the United States, going from success to success; in the face of such competition many British firms closed down and others were on the brink of collapse by the end of the 1960s.

One by one the big names disappeared, leaving specialist firms who survived by building small numbers of models, aimed at either racing or sports use. Their products were inevitably well made, well suited to their job, but expensive and appealing only to a limited market.

Norton and Triumph stayed in business through the 1970s, but Norton stopped building the Commando model in 1977 and Triumph's Meriden plant eventually ceased

production in the first few days of 1983. Norton returned to the marketplace in 1987 with a model powered by a rotary engine. This, in various forms, was built for six years before the firm collapsed.

Triumph turned out to be the success story of the 1990s. This was thanks to John Bloor who bought the name and created a new factory and modern model range that was launched late in 1990. It proved to be a winner, well able to compete with the best from Europe or Japan and the company is on course to continue this record of success into the next century.

Small firms, some still bearing the famous names of the past such as AJS and BSA, continued as a result of their high level of specialisation. Sales of new machines declined, but the boom in classic bikes which began around 1980 and focused heavily on British models, grew through that decade and into the next.

The British industry became a shadow of its former self, but the ghosts of the past took on a substantial form once they had been restored.

JAMES 1943 ML
James was one of the firms building light machines using 122cc Villiers engines in the late 1930s. They produced the Military Lightweight (ML) model, which was basic, cheap to make and suited to rapid troop dispersal. Sometimes dropped by parachute, it was called the 'Clockwork Mouse' by the army.

EXCELSIOR 1947 AUTOBYK
First seen in the late 1930s, these machines used a 98cc, single-speed Villiers engine. They fell out of favour with the public when mopeds became popular during the 1950s.

SCOTT 1949 FLYING SQUIRREL After the war, the Scott at first kept to girder forks but then changed to Dowty air suspension.

NORTON 1947 MANX
By the late-1930s the racing version of the camshaft Norton had developed into the Manx Grand Prix model. Postwar, as the Manx, it would be the mainstay of Norton's racing efforts. Given plunger suspension, it became known as the Garden Gate. It was built in 348cc and 498cc forms, the larger being the more successful. Both used the well-known, highly successful, single ohc engine designed by Arthur Carroll.

BSA 1950 A10 GOLDEN FLASH
In 1950 BSA introduced the 646cc A10 Golden Flash that copied the design of the A7 495cc twin, a model aiming to rival Triumph twin-cylinder machines. The model shown here is a 1952 A10 in the optional black finish; it was usually finished in golden beige.

BSA 1949 D1 BANTAM
This was one of BSA's most popular models. First seen in 1948 (123cc) as the D1 (above), it soon gained plunger rear suspension, a 148cc D3 version and competition models. The 123cc model was dropped after 1963 and a 172cc was introduced, which ran on up to 1971.

VELOCETTE 1949 LE
The LE was a highly innovative machine which marked a complete break with the firm's traditions. It had a 149cc engine which was enlarged to 192cc. It featured a flat-twin, side-valve, water-cooled engine, hand starter, hand gear change, beam frame, shaft drive and was incredibly quiet. The LE was intended to be a mass-market model, but was not cheap enough to succeed, although it remained in production up to 1970.

TRIUMPH 1949 TIGER 100
The sports Tiger 100 was introduced in 1939 and joined the Speed Twin in the Triumph range. The nacelle was introduced in 1949 for the headlamp and instruments and was used up to 1966. The black-and-silver finish of the Tiger was a smart contrast to the amaranth red of the Speed Twin.

NORTON 1953 DOMINATOR
Norton joined the twin-cylinder trend in 1949 with the 497cc model 7, designed by Bert Hopwood. The engine remained in production up to 1977, by which time it had been stretched to 829cc. At first the model used the existing frame with plunger rear suspension but this version had pivoted rear fork suspension and the pear-shaped silencers made their appearance.

JAMES 1949 COMET
After the war James continued with a policy of producing lightweight machines using Villiers engines. Next to the Autocycle, the most basic was the Comet which fitted the Villiers 1F engine of 99cc with a two-speed gearbox. This was controlled by a handlebar-mounted lever.

VINCENT-HRD 1949 RAPIDE
Early postwar Vincents used girder forks but were joined by the Series C in 1949 which featured the Girdraulic type. Phil Vincent had a poor opinion of telescopic forks so designed his to combine the rigidity of the girder with longer movement and hydraulic damping. The Rapide was capable of a modest 175 km/110 miles per hour.

VINCENT-HRD 1949 COMET
Vincent reintroduced a single-cylinder engine model in 1949. The rear cylinder of the twins was here replaced by a frame strut, and the integral gearbox changed to a separate Burman unit.

TRIUMPH 1950 THUNDERBIRD
For 1950 Triumph enlarged their twin to 649cc to introduce the Thunderbird to suit the demands of the American market. At the same time all the road models changed to a new tank style, adopted to help stop the chrome-plated ones from rusting as they crossed the Atlantic, while most had the sprung rear hub to give some degree of rear suspension.

BSA 1950 B31
After its 1945 introduction, the 348cc B31 changed little except for a plunger rear suspension option introduced in 1949. Later came a pivoted rear fork, but the B-range was altered little to the end of the 1950s.

CYCLEMASTER 1950
Not all clip-ons used a friction drive. This type, made by EMI, came as a complete wheel which simply replaced the bicycle one. It had a 26cc two-stroke, disc-valve engine later enlarged to all of 32cc. A two-stage chain drive took the power to the wheel.

BSA 1959 M21
The workhorse of the BSA range was the side-valve M-series models of which the 591cc M21 was the largest. They were mostly built as special orders for the AA which supplied them to their patrolmen

Built in the ligh

f Experience

THE UNAPPROACHABLE

Norton

THE WORLD'S BEST ROAD HOLDER

1954

NORTON 1952 DOMINATOR 88
This model married the Norton Dominator's 497cc twin engine to a Featherbed frame used by the Manx Norton, setting new standards for road holding for many years.

VINCENT 1953 FIREFLY
This 48cc two-stroke engine was initially listed by Vincent as a clip-on unit, and then as a complete machine using a special Sun bicycle. Its location meant that it had to be very narrow to allow the pedals to clear. It was made obsolete by the advent of the moped from Europe.

MATCHLESS 1953 G45
For road racing in the 500cc class Matchless chose to offer this twin to compete against the Manx Norton. It used a tuned version of the 498cc road twin engine mounted in the cycle parts of the 348cc 7R made by their AJS partners. This gave it good handling and brakes, but it was still outclassed by the Manx.

TRIUMPH 1954 TERRIER
Aimed at the lightweight market, the Terrier used a 149cc ohv engine with its four-speed gearbox unit. It had plunger rear suspension and was styled with nacelle and tank badges to ape the larger twins, a fine example of marketing. The Terrier ceased production in 1956.

MATCHLESS 1954 G80CS
AMC insisted on fitting their own rear units for many years, these being known as Jampots thanks to their shape.

TRIUMPH 1954 TR5 TROPHY
Triumph introduced the Trophy model in 1949 for road and competition use. One of their most successful and popular models, it combined low weight with easy handling so worked well in most situations. In modern times it would be called a trail bike but then it simply used the familiar 499cc twin engine tuned for a modest output to suit its use.

AMBASSADOR 1954 SUPREME
Based at Ascot in Surrey, this firm built small machines powered by Villiers engines from 1947 to 1964. The 1951 Supreme model was fitted with a 197cc 6E engine, and moved on to the 224cc 1H unit in 1954. It used pivoted-fork rear suspension.

WOOLER 1954
This interesting marque, first seen in 1911, always produced innovative if controversial designs. In 1954, they announced plans for a model using a flat-four engine, mounted in a frame with plunger rear suspension and telescopic forks. Sadly, it never did make it into production.

TRIUMPH 1955 SPEED TWIN By the middle of the decade the Speed Twin, and the other Triumph models, had moved on to pivoted-fork rear suspension but kept their style and fine lines. The model retained its amaranth red finish although the exact shade varied over the years.

ARIEL 1955 VB
Ariel were always a conservative marque, developing its products with gradual steps. By 1955 the 598cc side-valve single model VB had adopted pivoted-fork suspension, but its lines remained quite dated.

ROYAL ENFIELD 1955 BULLET
The Bullet name dated back to 1933 as sports models and postwar they were among the first to adopt rear suspension in 1949. The 346cc engine had the oil tank located at the rear of the crankcase and the gearbox bolted to that to form a single unit.

**DOUGLAS
1955 DRAGONFLY**
After the war Douglas introduced new models using a transverse, 348cc, ohv flat-twin. Built in touring and sports forms, short leading-link front forks and pivoted-rear suspension proved an excellent combination. In 1955 they were replaced by one model, the Dragonfly, featuring Earles forks and a fixed headlight. Production ceased in 1957.

VELOCETTE 1956 VENOM
The high-camshaft, overhead-valve Velocette models had their origins in the 1933 MOV of 248cc which was soon followed by 349cc and 495cc versions. In the 1950s, the two larger engines were joined by sports versions in 1956. The larger was the Venom which ran on to the end of the firm in 1971 in more than one guise.

MATCHLESS 1956 G9
AMC joined the move to twins in 1949 with the AJS model 20 and Matchless model G9. Both shared engines and most of the cycle parts although enthusiasts continued to exalt the prowess of one over the other for years despite them coming off the same production line. Aside from having a third main bearing, the engines were conventional as were the machines but they had style, speed and were popular.

FRANCIS-BARNETT 1956 CRUISER 75
The advent of the 224cc Villiers 1H engine with its smooth shape and apparent unit construction enabled firms such as Francis-Barnett to move on from the 197cc models. This was one result, the model 75 built from 1954 to 1957 by a firm that had a reputation of building lightweights which were that little bit better than average.

TRIUMPH 1957 CUB
The Terrier grew up to become the 199cc Cub. In 1957 it adopted pivoted-fork rear suspension and was joined by a competition version, the first of several. The Cub, always a popular model, was kept in production by Triumph up to 1968.

GREEVES 1957
Most Greeves models were for competition, but they also built road machines such as this. It retained the famous cast-alloy frame beam and the leading-link front forks, being powered by a 197cc Villiers 9E engine. Later came versions using 250cc single or twin-cylinder engines.

TRIUMPH 1957 TWENTY-ONE
This was the first of the unit-construction twins. It had a 349cc engine which followed the Triumph format but the stylish rear enclosure was new – the shape quickly led to it being named the 'bathtub'. This one is a very early model which was to be followed by a 490cc version in Speed Twin and sports forms.

ARIEL 1958 LEADER
Staid and conservative Ariel shattered the British market when they introduced the Leader in 1958. Totally new and completely different from their four-stroke range with its twin-cylinder, two-stroke engine, beam frame and full enclosure, it was modern in style and engineering; in effect a scooter with large wheels.

EXCELSIOR 1958 SUPER TALISMAN TWIN
This firm differed from most who produced lightweights in that they built their own engines as well as using Villiers ones. For their 1950 twin they designed their own 243cc unit which was joined later by this 328cc model, both to run on into the early 1960s.

BSA 1958 D5 BANTAM
Having stretched the Bantam to 148cc and then fitted it into a frame with pivoted-fork rear suspension, BSA opened the engine out to 172cc to create the D5. It used the older frame and was only built for the one year, being superseded by the 172cc D7 in 1959, this using the same engine in a new frame. In this form it ran on to 1971, becoming the D10, D14 and D175 in the process and gaining a much needed four-speed gearbox along the way.

BSA 1960 GOLDEN FLASH A10
For its final years the A10 lost its all-beige finish, but gained a headlamp nacelle and full-width hubs for both wheels. A popular model in all its forms, it was replaced by a new series in 1962 but these lacked some of the style of the old type.

TRIUMPH 1960 TROPHY TR6
The larger 649cc Trophy model was derived from the original but this was to be its last year for the era of large off-road machines was ending. For 1961 the TR6 returned but as a road model, effectively a Bonneville with just one carburettor which gave it a good performance with smooth running.

BSA 1962 ROCKET GOLD STAR
The pinnacle of the early BSA twin series was this super-sports machine, essentially the Rocket engine in the Gold Star cycle parts. Only built for two years, it became one of the most desirable of classic motorcycles. Super Rocket models could be made to look similar but were never quite the same thing.

FRANCIS-BARNETT 1960 TRIALS 85
For the 1960s this firm, along with James a part of the AMC group, was instructed to fit AMC engines rather than the traditional Villiers to its frame. This change did not prove to be a success although this trials model, fitted with the 249cc capacity engine, did have the benefit of Norton forks. By 1963 it was back to a Villiers engine.

FRANCIS-BARNETT 1962 FULMAR
Introduced to bring a radical change in style to the lightweight machine, the Fulmar had a spine frame built up from tubing under its body work. The fuel tank was located under the seat so the dummy one was used for stowage. The engine was the 149cc AMC unit but this was by then being assembled by Villiers so much improved.

JAMES 1963 CADET
Restyled for 1963, and actually based on the Francis-Barnett Plover model, the Cadet continued to do the same unglamorous job it had held down from 1949, taking people about their business. In this form it used the 149cc AMC engine unit rather than the 122cc Villiers of the past but was replaced by the conventional M16 model in 1965.

JAMES
1963 SUPERSWIFT
James did not list a postwar twin until this model appeared in 1962, to be joined by a sports version the next year. Both fitted the Villiers 249cc twin-cylinder engine, allegedly tuned for the sports model, and handsome in this blue and silver. The sports model lost the enclosed chain drive but gained a flyscreen.

BSA 1963 B40 STAR
In 1958 BSA launched their unit-construction single, the 247cc C15. It was to grow into a whole series and in 1961 was joined by the 343cc B40, both versions also appearing in sports guise as the SS80 and SS90. Later still came 441cc models for road and trail use, and finally a full 499cc machine.

TRIUMPH 1963
BONNEVILLE T120
The larger 649cc twins changed to unit construction in 1963 and the cult sports model of the era became the twin-carburettor Bonneville. Fast and most successful in production racing, it was offered in off-road forms in the United States and also as the single-carburettor TR6 Trophy. This is the 1970 version.

VELOCETTE 1967 THRUXTON
Velocette kept to their traditional singles right to the end,
even when the public turned to the bigger twins which were
easier to ride fast. The sports 499cc Venom continued to
offer performance to keep the 650s on their toes and the
final outcome was the Thruxton to which was added this
stylish fairing.

BSA 1969 BANTAM BUSHMAN
When the D10 Bantam arrived in 1966 it was offered in four
forms, two of which had the new four-speed gearbox and
one of these was the Bushman model, aimed at the trail
bike market. It continued as a D14 and then in this final
form using the well-developed 172cc engine.

117

BSA 1969 ROCKET 3
Also introduced as the Triumph Trident, with a differing engine and
frame, the Rocket 3 was a great motorcycle whose engine design
owed much to the Triumph twin. On the road it proved fast and highly
capable, it was the machines' hard luck that they appeared just as the
Japanese moved into the large-capacity sector of the market.

MATCHLESS
1987 ROADSTER
Built by the same firm that kept the Triumph name in public view in the 1980s, the Matchless fitted a 494cc Austrian Rotax engine unit in conventional cycle parts which gave the machine a classic line. Sold to that market, by 1990 it was being built in small number to special order, no doubt until stocks were used up.

TRITON
The idea of combining the merits of the fine handling of the Norton featherbed frame with the easily-tuned Triumph twin engine first occurred in the 1950s when it was possible to get Manx Nortons minus engine and gearbox easily. Later the idea became the cult Café Racer and continued through the 1960s and beyond. This one uses the three-cylinder Trident engine.

QUASAR 1978
Very different and created by Malcolm Newell to show his theories for feet-forward machines, the Quasar used a 848cc Reliant car engine and had special features to enhance rider comfort. Built in small numbers in the late 1970s, it created a vogue of its own, but later attempts to build similar concepts failed to find buyers.

NORTON 1971 COMMANDO ROADSTER
The Commando was launched in 1967 with a 745cc Norton twin engine, and featured an Isolastic system to insulate the rider from engine vibration through the use of rubber mountings for engine, gearbox and rear fork. It was soon joined by other versions while the engine was enlarged to 829cc in 1973.

RICKMAN ENFIELD 1971
The combination of the tough Royal Enfield Interceptor II 736cc twin-cylinder engine and the immaculate frame built by the Rickman brothers resulted in this handsome machine. It came about as the old company fell on hard times and was one of the last of a line of fine, lusty machines which performed well but needed some muscle to keep them in check.

HESKETH 1982 V1000
Launched at a garden party held at Lord Hesketh's estate, this massive machine was conventional but complex and expensive. Its 992cc V-twin engine had overhead camshafts, four valves per cylinder and a fine frame. The suspension, instruments and much else had to be imported but its real problem lay in some gearbox faults which took time to rectify before production could begin.

**ENFIELD
1991 BULLET 500**
In 1956 Royal Enfield set up a factory in India to build their 350 Bullet model to sell there. The project proved a success, was separated from Redditch, and in 1977 the Indian Bullets began to be imported back into Britain. They had changed little and now there are several models listed, including this larger 499cc one.

NORTON 1988 COMMANDER
In the 1970s Norton inherited a rotary engine project but it was 1988 before a road machine appeared, at first air-cooled. Then came this water-cooled model, fully equipped with fairing and panniers for modern riding, which found favour with owners who enjoyed its totally smooth engine and fine handling. Sadly, attempts to build on this good start came to nothing despite racing successes and resultant sports models.

NORTON 1974 JOHN PLAYER COMMANDO
To take advantage of sponsorship from the tobacco company, this model was built for just one year, fitting the 829cc engine. The body style set it off from most machines then on the road and it was strictly for a rider only.

TRIUMPH 1971 TRIDENT
The Trident was given the new group forks and hubs for 1971 but this did not stop it being a great motorcycle. That year the company had many racing successes with the model which continued in production to 1976, although the final version used the BSA Rocket 3 engine with its inclined cylinders.

TRIUMPH 1994 TIGER 900
Introduced for 1993, the successful Tiger 900 was a trail or off-road version of the Trident which used a detuned version of the engine in a strengthened frame of extended wheelbase and fitted with wire wheels, radial tyres and a half fairing.

BSA 1971 THUNDERBOLT
For 1971 BSA and Triumph had a major new model
combined launch from which they ran into many troubles.
The big twins such as this Thunderbolt had a new frame
which pushed the seat height to an unacceptable level.
Forks, wheel hubs and many details were also new and
shared by both firms and the result for BSA was collapse in
a year or so.

TRIUMPH 1995 THUNDERBIRD
For 1995 Triumph brought back an old and loved name from the classic era along with one of their 1950s tank badges to create their own classic model using the favourite 885cc three-cylinder engine. A great combination of old and new it showed that the British industry was far from down and out. Triumph at Hinckley is one of the success stories of today.

ENFIELD & WATSONIAN 1995
Watsonian continued to offer traditional sidecars as well as later styles over the years. In this case their GP Jubilee Classic model is hitched to an Indian Enfield to which it matches well in form and colour.

127

EUROPE: THE SPECIALISTS

BMW 1923 R32

The European motorcycling industry took its first steps in 1894 when Hildebrand & Wolfmüller established a factory in Munich to make motorcycles. Unfortunately, this machine was unreliable, and the company soon closed.

While Germany took the commercial lead, in France and Italy there were also experiments with the new technology. Frenchman Félix Théodore Millet developed a five-cylinder radial engine initially located in the front wheel, and later moved to the rear. Despite the inherent problems with this layout, the machine worked, but also proved unreliable. In Italy, Enrico Bernardi mounted a single-cylinder, water-cooled 265cc engine on a platform, fitted a single wheel, and attached it to a bicycle. It was the first Italian motorcycle and had overhead valves, possibly the first in the world and a foretaste of the obsession Italian manufacturers have with performance.

The excellent de Dion-Bouton engine and the stable tricycle layout proved a popular combination for several years.

HILDEBRAND & WOLFMÜLLER 1895
Thought to be the first commercially produced motorcycle, this had an open frame and a twin-cylinder, water-cooled engine with pistons connected directly to the rear wheel.

WERNER 1901
The first machines built by the Werner Fréres had the engine mounted above the front wheel, making the centre of gravity too high for easy control. In 1901 they moved the engine to a central position with the crankcase bolted into the frame and the cylinder upright. Thus, the basic design was established as shown in this 1903 advertisement.

FLOTTWEG 1921
This German firm went into business producing this 119cc attachment engine along with a bicycle to suit. The side-valve engine drove the wheel by chain and the magneto fitted behind the headstock. They were popular for short period, but were generally ridden until they broke down and then discarded.

LAURIN & KLEMENT 1905
Initially built in Austria, this brand was typical of European design in the Edwardian period. The magneto hung under the crankcase (the alternative was above the engine) and protected by a full frame loop that ran underneath. The V-twin engine fitted snugly within the basic frame design and became the popular alternative to the single.

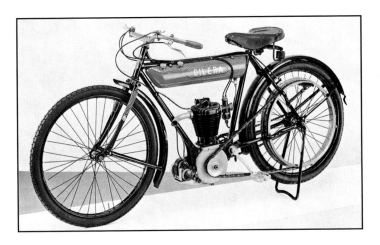

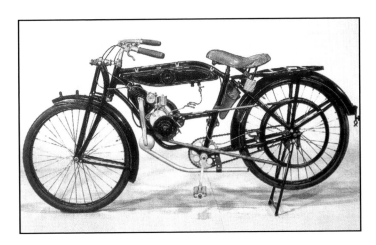

GILERA 1909
A major Italian firm founded by Giuseppe Gilera who built this first machine with a 317cc side-valve engine, direct-belt drive, magneto ignition and sprung forks to compete in a hill climb. There was limited production at first, but the firm took off in the 1920s after it moved to Arcore.

FN 1914
This Belgian firm was famous on two counts: they offered an in-line four as well as a single, and they employed shaft drive at a time when the belt drive was the norm. However, the brakes and suspension were basic and in the 1920s the firm changed to chain drive to cut costs.

BMW 1923 R32
The first true BMW motorcycle had a flat-twin engine, built in unit with its gearbox and shaft-drive like the modern models. This original design was used 60 years before the firm changed to another layout.

DKW 1922 REICHSFAHRTMODELL
Famous for their two-stroke engines, this German firm began with an attachment above the rear wheel and then moved within the frame. The capacity was 143cc with fan cooling, enclosed cylinder, flywheel magneto ignition and petroil lubrication.

MOTO GUZZI 1924
This Italian firm, always innovative, began in 1921 building machines with a horizontal single-cylinder engine, an external flywheel and overhead valves. This successful early racing model had an overhead camshaft and four valves.

131

DKW 1925 SM
This engine of this model was enlarged from the 143cc used by the Reichsfahrtmodell to 175cc, but the real innovation was the frame. It was a single pressed-steel beam with added members (shown here). It was not built in large numbers, but the pressed steel revealed a design trend that would be more widely adopted in Europe over the next

JAWA 1929 500 OHV
This Czechoslovakian firm started producing motorcycles by building the German Wanderer design under license. The result was this 500cc, single-cylinder, ohv engine in unit with the gearbox and shaft drive. The frame and the leaf-sprung, trailing-link front fork were in pressed-steel, but the model was not a success.

BMW 1931 R11
For the 1930s, pressed-steel frames and forks were used in a style common in Europe. Both side-valve and overhead-valve engines were in use in 500cc and 750cc sizes by then. A 250cc single was created from the twins.

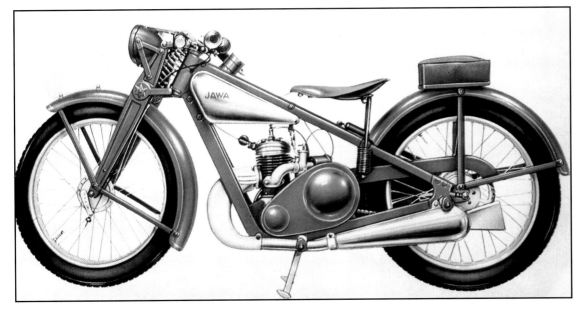

JAWA 1932 175
This simple machine used a 2-stroke engine and a pressed-steel frame with girder forks. The result was cheap and reliable, and could be tuned by novice racers – factors that turned it into a commercial success.

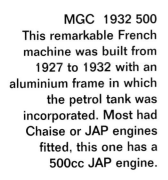

MGC 1932 500
This remarkable French machine was built from 1927 to 1932 with an aluminium frame in which the petrol tank was incorporated. Most had Chaise or JAP engines fitted, this one has a 500cc JAP engine.

MOTO GUZZI 1933 GT17
This model retained the early Moto Guzzi feature of the overhead inlet valve and side exhaust. This one is fitted for military use, one of a number of variations the firm offered the services.

PUCH 1934 250S4
Puch, an old-established Austrian firm, usually built two-stroke engines, but often of the split-single type with the crankshaft running along the frame, such as this example. This unconventional approach extended to a direct bevel drive to the gearbox with the clutch located in the rear wheel hub.

The Werner was available at the same time. It had a belt-driven engine mounted above the front wheel. This location made the machine top-heavy, so grip in wet conditions was difficult and a fall usually meant a fire from the hot-tube ignition system.

Generally, progress in motorcycling was held back but this was slowly overcome as the industry developed. By 1901 Werner Frères had moved the engine to the central position in the frame and, although not the first to use it, patented this design. The tricycle with its three tracks was extremely uncomfortable to ride over the poor road surfaces, so motorcyclists turned to the two-wheeled, single-tracked solo in the early 1900s. A passenger sidecar was soon added and the combination proved far superior to the previous forecar or trailer concepts. Other firms began to produce engines for motorcycles and competition between manufacturers became fierce as many new brands appeared all over Europe.

France was the major motorcycle manufacturer at that time; it was also the home of long-distance races between towns such as Paris-to-Bordeaux. At first motorcycles were raced as a class at major car events, as tricycles had previously. The last inter-town race took place in 1903 and was from Paris to Madrid. However, it was stopped at Bordeaux after many fatal accidents involving competitors and spectators; Bucquet and his Werner made the fastest time and averaged 60 km/37 miles per hour.

The move to circuit racing led to the International Cup races, open to national teams of three, and run from 1904 to 1906. Sadly, the first was a fiasco, the results declared void; the second and third were full of protests, but from this, the idea of a Tourist Trophy or TT was born in 1907.

In spite of manufacturers introducing many new engine designs for the public to sample, the popularity of motorcycles faltered up to 1910. France was usually at the cutting edge, but they gradually took a lesser role in the development of the industry. The German industry recovered from a period of decline to compete with Austria, Belgium, Italy and Switzerland for sales but, as the First World War drew near, Britain became the major European

NSU 1934 OSL 251
During the 1930s this German firm built a range of singles with the oil tank incorporated in front of the crankcase. Full chaincases and camshaft engines were a feature in a period when most motorcycles used pushrods. The works racers were more exotic, using supercharged twin-cylinder engines with twin overhead camshafts, but failed to succeed on the circuits.

DKW 1935 SB 500 DE LUXE
The SB series had introduced the important Schnürle loop-scavenging principles for two-stroke engines in 1932 and they used them to very good effect. The de luxe version of this model featured it along with an electric starter, twin headlamps and an instrument panel mounted on the handlebars.

135

GILERA 1936 LTE
Gilera continued to produce their vintage-style singles into the 1930s and for the armed forces during the war. They were rugged, sturdy and the pivoted-fork rear suspension made them comfortable. This machine was appropriate for civilian and service use.

NIMBUS 1936
Denmark's major firm built four-cylinder shaft drive machines from 1920 to 1957. They ceased production in 1928, but began again in 1934 when they changed to ohc engines and rigid frames, still in the flat steel strips of earlier models (shown here). They even fitted telescopic forks in 1934, before BMW. This was a bizarre combination of old and modern technology.

manufacturer. Italy produced motorcycles for its home market, although Central European countries used motorcycles from their neighbouring countries.

The First World War delayed developments as motorcycle manufacturers turned to making armaments. After the war new firms sprang up all over the world, but demand for machines outstripped what could be built. Shortages, rationing and strikes all caused bottlenecks, but the French, Belgian and Italian industries were able to supply the marketplace once they had reorganised.

In Germany, where political disorder and runaway inflation persisted well into the 1920s, it took a great deal of effort and ingenuity to produce machines at all. Despite this, the demand for transport encouraged many new firms to start up, often using a bought-in engine for their limited production. One such company was BMW who in 1923 launched their famous flat twin which has been built using the original concept to this day.

Italy saw the birth of the Moto Guzzi company, which built machines radical in design, yet always functional with a unique line and style. There were plenty of other firms that supplied the needs of a populace who seemed to

love all forms of transport. Gilera, Benelli and Bianchi were all prewar firms but Garelli, MM and many others appeared in the 1920s. While some enjoyed success for years, others became victims of the Depression.

The Italian firms enjoyed a home market which was keen to ride and race, so efforts to export were limited. This isolation did not impede their technical innovation. The classic transverse four raced in the late 1930s by Gilera, and from 1950 to 1976 by MV Agusta, had its origins in a design from the 1920s. In 1930, Moto Guzzi had a similar engine, but laid horizontal and supercharged.

The industry had now spread across Europe, and other countries began to build rather than import. Austria had been involved since the beginning of motorcycle manufacture but other firms appeared in Czechoslovakia, Hungary and Poland, Denmark, Sweden and the Netherlands. Some used imported engines and parts, others manufactured whole motorcycles.

In road racing, Some of the other European manufacturers offered fierce competition to the successful tradition established by British firms. Peugeot of France used an overhead-camshaft twin, Bianchi from Italy used a similar

DKW 1936 NZ350
A prewar model, shown here in military finish. It had a conventional 346cc two-stroke engine with a four-speed gearbox. It was also built in a 247cc size and after 1944 the 350cc replaced the complex BMW and Zundapp sidecar outfits, because it was cheaper and easier to produce.

GILERA 1938 GIGANTE VT
Gilera, like other Italian firms, built a range of load-carrying three-wheel motorcycles by connecting an existing machine with a variety of trailers, in this case the 498cc or 582cc ohv single. They had four speeds, shaft drive to the rear axle and disc wheels.

single and both achieved success between the wars. The German manufacturers – BMW, DKW and NSU – were all competitive in their class and there were many more that had a brief moment of glory on the winners' dais.

At the end of the 1920s a new frame design appeared in Europe using pressed-steel in place of tubing. This meant the petrol tank was placed between the upper part of the motorcycle which gave it a new line and style. However, this new design was not universally adopted, but mainly used by BMW and Zundapp, also by firms from neighbouring countries.

The Depression affected firms in Europe in the same way as the rest of the world. Many companies closed down in the early 1930s, but political events brought major changes.

In Italy, Mussolini pushed the industry forward and aided the expansion of the home market by making small machines exempt from tax. It was much the same in Germany once Hitler was in power, because the government percieved that by encouraging motorcycling, the population would become trained in riding and mainte-

nance, useful attributes to an army turning to mechanised transport. Thus, lightweights, considered cheap transport and an effective use of materials in manufacture and operation, went untaxed.

Both Italy and Germany had massive propaganda machines and sought success in racing as a means of promoting national esteem. From the middle of the 1930s the effects of this policy became more evident. Italy set the pace in 1930 and 1931 when they won the International Six Days' Trophy, but Germany took over from 1933 to 1935. Moto Guzzi shattered British conceptions by winning two TTs in 1935 and another in 1937 while German DKWs began to be the most successful in 250cc races.

Record-breaker Ernst Henne had already given notice of his abilities by setting a new motorcycle world speed record back in 1929 on a BMW. He then set new records no less than six times from 1930 to 1937, the final figure standing until 1951. BMW gradually improved their flat twin for racing and were most successful in 1938. In 1939 they added a Senior TT win to their tally, but overall, the best that year was an Italian Gilera four. That same Gilera, fully streamlined, briefly held the outright record in 1937, subject to a dispute, but Henne settled the matter by raising the figure further. Gilera claimed a place in the record books by covering over 205 km/127 miles in an hour running up and down an autostrada and held that title until 1953.

During the Second World War most motorcycles used by the armed forces were based on civilian models, but in Belgium the three major firms – FN, Gillet and Sarolea – all built sidecar outfits designed to cope with the mud of Flanders. Once their factories were occupied, they produced machines for the Germans who scrutinised the technical specifications to improve their own models.

From this came the complex BMW and Zundapp flat twins with their dual-range plus reverse gearboxes, sidecar-wheel drive and a locking differential. They worked well in the right hands but were costly to build and the drivers required special training.

After the war came the problems of reconstruction following the devastation of so much industrial plant. In general, most countries chose to produce small-capacity models, usually two-strokes. These modest machines were cheap and easy to get into production to satisfy the urgent need for transport.

Italy was fortunate in that only the Benelli factory had suffered any serious damage, so its industry recovered faster than most. Racing quickly followed, a major factor being the introduction of the scooter which rapidly became an important sector of the market. Alongside the scooter, many people turned to tiny-capacity models as an aid to travel. The appearance of these small capacity machines introduced a large number of people to motorcycling.

In Germany the population worked furiously to bring order from chaos, despite the division of the country, the presence of the occupying troops and the many restrictions. By 1950 the situation had changed, they had become a major exhibitor at European shows; the German economic miracle was now in full swing.

Manufacturers in France and the Benelux countries concentrated on producing cyclemotors and small two-strokes. Both benefited from tax and insurance concessions and proved highly popular. In Spain stability came to an industry established by means of import restrictions that kept the competition at bay. From this the practice of Spanish firms making foreign parts or machines under licence with Ducati, Villiers and Amal began.

The 1950s were a period of stability and European firms were able to advance technically and show innovative designs and ideas at shows across the Continent. Mopeds replaced cyclemotors in many areas. The NSU Quickly was one of the first. It was very successful and was little more difficult to handle than a bicycle. More and more scooters appeared and in Italy the practice of offering one basic model in a series of forms ranging from tourer to racer proved popular.

The German industry ran into problems, despite the success of the firms building mopeds. They expanded too quickley and were caught out by a market that suddenly declined. In the middle of the decade the country's economic success led people to move on from the two wheels they had to the four they desired and could now afford. The motorcycle manufacturers were not ready for this, and a difficult few years resulted in the demise of many firms.

The 1950s saw the end of the domination of the British made machines in road racing. The Italian Gilera, Moto Guzzi and then the MV Agusta were the successes in the

JAWA 1937 ROBOT
The most basic model in the range was simple, easy to maintain and repair, and cheap enough to discard if anything major went wrong.

PUCH 1938 350GS
Similar in layout to the 250S4, this machine differed in that the cylinder bores were staggered to give the split-single cylinder offset effect. It also had an ingenious link rear suspension although the machines built for army use had rigid frames.

350cc and 500cc classes. BMW ruled the sidecar roost from 1955, winning virtually all the classic races for the rest of the decade. Italy dominated the 125cc and 250cc classes mainly because of Mondial and MV Agusta, plus Benelli and Moto Guzzi in the earlier years. Only in 1953 and 1954 did they have real opposition, which came from an NSU team with their sophisticated four-strokes,

Europe, like the rest of the world, was affected by the emergence of the Japanese industry in the 1960s, so some barriers to trade were imposed. These did not halt the decline of the late 1950s from continuing throughout the 1960s, although some companies were assisted by their government relaxing tax and license regulations. Many firms went to the wall, but new manufacturers started up, some of which remain into the 1990s.

The Japanese came to dominate racing although MV Agusta held on to the 500cc class and BMW the sidecar class. After 1967 Honda and Suzuki stopped competing, which led to a revival of MV Agusta's dominance of the 350cc class, while the Spain's Derbi and Italy's Benelli had success in the 50cc and 250cc classes respectively.

The firms that survived into the 1970s soon found they were in a boom period again, as a result of spiralling fuel prices and increased traffic congestion. Most of the new business went to the Japanese manufacturers, but mopeds, scooters and, in Italy, small motorcycles all sold well. This led to the introduction of some interesting large models. Companies such as Benelli, Ducati and Moto Guzzi all introduced large-capacity machines while BMW produced a new range of their traditional flat twins. These later led to the fully-faired motorcycle format.

There were changes on the racing scene. The Japanese took over from MV Agusta in the larger classes and from BMW in the sidecar class. The 250cc class was mainly shared by Yamaha and Kawasaki, but in the middle of the decade Harley-Davidson dominated for three years, using Italian-built Aermacchi machines. The 50cc and 125cc classes were shared between European firms from Spain, Germany and Italy, the Spanish being the most successful.

The global recession of the early 1980s caused a gradual fall in sales. European motorcycles became less competitive compared with the new range of large, well-built, sophisticated Japanese models that handled well. Despite the economic climate, BMW chose to launch a completely new model type in 1983, one that was far removed from their flat twin and sufficiently different from the Japanese models to make it stand out.

The classic bike revival initially grew at a much faster pace in Britain. This soon changed. There were shows and events all over Europe, with interesting and obscure models from the past. In addition to parades and races for owners of classic machines, organisers added the regularity run where the aim was to lap a circuit consistently. Owners of rare machines could give them a competitive airing without overstraining them more than they wished.

The popularity of classic bikes increased into the 1990s as new sales declined. European firms took the lead and pulled business back from the Japanese. Their innovation succeeded and, with new designs from BMW, Aprilia, Cagiva, Ducati and specialists such as Bimota, appealed to buyers. New sales therefore increase once again.

DKW 1939 RT 125
This model was first seen in 1935 and had a conventional two-stroke engine built into a unit with a three-speed gearbox. During the postwar period it was copied many times: as the BSA Bantam, the Harley-Davidson Hummer, the Yamaha Red Dragonfly, the Russian Voskhod and it remained in production as the IFA.

FN 1938 M-12
This example was built for the armed forces and based on the civilian model. It had to cope with the mud of Flanders, and therefore was given a 992cc flat-twin, side-valve engine, a four-speed with reverse gearbox, and shaft drive. This machine was also used as the basis of a tricar for general load carriage.

PUCH 1939 125
This far more conventional Puch retained the split-single cylinder engine, built into a unit with a three-speed gearbox, that had the clutch positioned between the two. This motorcycle was still produced in the postwar period.

MOTO GUZZI 1940 TRIALCE
Here the front end of the Alce model was attached to a rear section that had twin driven wheels. These were built to carry stores, ammunition and heavy machine guns (shown here). The engine was the stock 500cc single.

GILERA 1941 MARTE
Intended as a sidecar machine, the Marte used the 498cc side-valve engine with a shaft-driven rear wheel. The wheel of the sidecar, which had suspension, could be driven by a shaft that ran across from the motorcycle. Thus, Gilera alone solved the problem of both suspending and driving the rear and sidecar wheels.

BMW 1941 R75
BMW built this complex motorcycle for the armed forces. It had a flat-twin, 745cc ohv engine, four-speed gearbox with high and low, forward and reverse ratios. There was also a bevel box with lockable differential and a drive to the side-car wheel. The machine was massive, used on most fronts and needed skill to drive.

ZUNDAPP 1941 KS750
This massive outfit was built to be the equivalent of the BMW. It could also be connected to the same sidecar with the driven wheel. The KS750 had a V-twin engine (170-degree *V*, almost a flat-twin), four-speed gearbox, with high and low plus reverse ratios and a lockable differential. The front forks are actually girders, not telescopics.

MOTO GUZZI 1946 SUPERALCE
Introduced after the war for military and law enforcement use. The Superalce was used into the 1950s and had overhead valves but kept the girder forks. Most were built as solos, but there were a few made with sidecars (shown here).

JAWA 1946 250
Much of the design of this machine was carried out during the Nazi occupation in secrecy. The result was this 250cc two-stroke with single cylinder, unit construction, telescopic forks and plunger rear suspension.

VESPA 1946
The first scooters were a 1920s fad, but in 1946 the Piaggio Vespa (the Italian for wasp) was introduced and became a great success. It had small wheels, an open frame, weather protection and the mechanics were hidden. The scooter appealed to a new market and Vespa became synonymous with scooter.

BMW 1949 R24
The first postwar model was this 247cc single that used the same concept of unit construction and shaft drive as the twins. It gained plunger rear suspension the following year, so was the last BMW to lack that feature. The single was produced up to 1967, when it had become too expensive for the market.

NSU 1953 QUICKLY
From 1936 NSU built the 98cc Quick, but this was replaced in 1953 by this model, which set the style for mopeds for years to come. Well built, easy to ride, simple to maintain, the machine was produced in large numbers and found a ready market.

MOTO GUZZI 1949 GTV
This was the last year for this long-running model which then became the Falcone. Both models had the traditional horizontal, 499cc, ohv engine in the style the firm used for so long.

145

IFA 1953 RT125
After the war the old DKW works found itself in East Germany and became known as IFA. The 125cc simply ran on with just a tank badge change and the addition of plunger rear suspension (shown here).

BMW 1955 R50 & R69
In 1955 the firm adopted pivoted-fork rear suspension, by modifying the existing frame design. They also fitted Earles leading-link forks and this design was used up to 1969. These two models were joined by the sports R50S and R69S, plus the detuned R60. The 247cc single was modified in the same way.

ISO 1955 125 ISOMOTO
Bubble cars, luxury cars, scooters and motorcycles have all been produced by this Italian firm. This model used a split-single, two-stroke engine in a scooter-style frame. An interesting concept, it showed the company's breadth of vision.

BMW 1960 R50
This is the basic small touring twin which delivered surprising performance in near silence. All BMWs of the period had this attribute, but the touring models were especially quiet. This example is finished in traditional black and white.

NSU 1955 SPORTSMAX
The Max had a 247cc, single-cylinder engine with a over-head camshaft driven by a system of eccentrics and connecting rods similar to some car engines of the 1920s. It worked well and the Max and Supermax were good road machines from which the highly successful, road-racing Sportsmax was developed.

149

CAPRIOLO 1956 125
An Italian firm that adopted the German or Czech style of pressed-steel frames for early-postwar models. The engine had an overhead camshaft, but this was a face camshaft located at the top of the vertical shaft. It was neat and proved successful.

MOTO GUZZI 1961 MULO MECCANICO
This bizarre vehicle used the original engine type now found in the modern Guzzi. It was built for the armed forces and was able to go over any terrain. It had a 754cc V-twin, ohv engine of limited power and great torque.

150

PROGRESS 1957
This scooter was a
German design, normally
powered by a Sachs
engine, but they were
also made in Britain
under licence where they
had Villiers engines.

DUCATI 1963
200 SUPER SPORTS
This is a typical example
of the early overhead-
camshaft Ducati singles.
Built for many years in a
variety of sizes and
degrees of tuning, the
Mach 1 became a cult
model.

BMW 1969 R75/5
The modern BMW twin
can be said to have been
derived from the /5
machines. They had major
engine changes, new
cycle parts and a revised
image. The range was
soon extended from the
first three models of
498cc, 599cc and 746cc
capacity, listed as the
R50/5, R60/5 and this
R75/5.

BENELLI 1967 BARACUDA
This firm was founded by six brothers in 1911 who built many fine machines for road or competition. However, this one is really a Motobi, a firm set up by one of the six who returned to the fold. His Motobi models were then given Benelli badges.

MV AGUSTA 1969 750 SPORT
MV exhibited a road four at a Milan show in 1950, but it was 1965 before the first road 600cc went on sale as a tourer. However, in 1970 the 743cc Sport model appeared with shaft drive and the styling of the racing fours. It was expensive and fast, the Ferrari of the two-wheels.

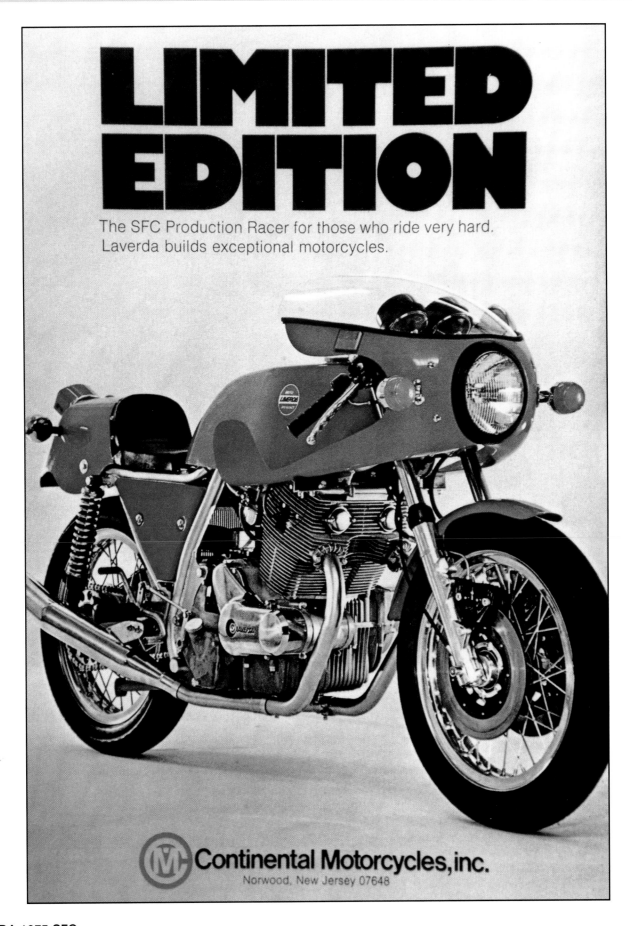

LAVERDA 1975 SFC
This Italian firm moved into the sports market with their 744cc twin – a very tough, fast machine with good handling, available with higher states of tuning. The SFC version (shown here), was in effect a production racer that was road-legal.

153

GILERA 1972 TRIAL 50
A very typical small Italian motorcycle. Most firms produced similar machines in road and trail formats all based on the same 50cc engine and gearbox package (shown here). Sometimes tuned differently to suit the intended use.

CASAL 1972 PHANTOM 5
Built in Portugal, this model was part of a range of 50cc capacity motorcycles, aimed mainly at the young rider or commuter. This was a sports moped fitted with a five-speed gearbox and other features taken from larger and faster models.

MZ 1974 TS 150
This model had East German origins yet was popular. The MZ introduced a great deal of modern two-stroke technology. The rear chain case includes rubber enclosures.

BMW 1975 R90S
The familiar flat-twin was increased to a 898cc model with bigger carburettors, and cockpit fairing. The result was a fast road machine that was also comfortable over long distances. The twin discs were a useful asset as were the powerful horns.

155

DKW 1975 HERCULES WANKEL
Sold in the United Kingdom as a DKW, this rotary-engined machine was a Hercules W2000. Although a technical innovation, the high fuel consumption and price were not balanced by good performance.

PUCH 1975 MAXI S
The simple Maxi was built in several forms, most of which sold extremely well during the 1970s. Easy to ride, economical, with adequate performance from the 50cc two-stroke engine and easy to service; they were very popular.

VESPA 1975 200 RALLY
By the 1970s, when the Vespa scooter had reached this style, little had altered from the original. Only Lambretta offered any real competition.

MOTO GUZZI
1975 850-T3
The V-twin, ohv engine from the service vehicle went on to power many Guzzi models including this one. Common to most was a linked braking system, whereby the foot pedal operated the rear brake and one front disc, the hand lever operated the second front disc; the system was very effective.

DERBI 1975 GT
This 50cc sports model was built by a Spanish firm that was a successful Grand Prix contender in the smaller classes. The four-speed gearbox and stylish lines ensured its popularity with young Spaniards.

GITANE 1975 COMFORT
A typical French moped built in considerable numbers and in several formats with style and flair. It had a two-stroke engine, 50cc, automatic transmission and simple controls.

BATAVUS 1976 STARGLO
This firm was founded in 1904 and builds mopeds in a variety of formats, most of which are based on a simple 50cc two-stroke engine with automatic transmission. Basic but popular.

COSSACK 1977 650D
In contrast to the BMW, the USSR's Cossack was sold for both solo and sidecar use. They were based on old BMWs captured during the war and achieved some popularity, partly as a result of their low cost.

BMW 1976 R100RS
BMW moved ahead of their rivals in 1976 with this model, complete with the stylish fairing as standard. Developed in a wind tunnel, it allowed the rider to cruise at a steady 160 km/100 miles per hour, neatly tracked in with a fuel stop every 320 km/200 miles. Dropped in 1983, public demand forced its return.

COSSACK 1975 PLANETA
A range of two-stroke machines from the USSR were imported into the United Kingdom during the 1970s. This example had a 350cc single-cylinder engine, others had 125cc or 175cc unit engines. There was also a 350cc twin and sidecar outfits.

MORINI 1977 3½ SPORT An Italian firm that began with two-strokes, moved on to overhead camshafts and quick racers before turning to the V-twin engine. This was built mainly in 344cc and 479cc capacities, although there was a 240cc model, but that proved too expensive to achieve high sales. Otherwise this was a popular twin with enthusiasts.

MOBYLETTE 1976

A very long-running French moped, built in large numbers and sold worldwide. It had a basic 50cc two-stroke engine and automatic transmission with fixed or variable ratios. This made it easy to ride and to maintain.

CZ 1977 125/175 DE LUXE

This Czechoslovakian motorcycle was built in two capacities. The features included pumped lubrication for the two-stroke engine, a gear lever that doubled as the kickstarter and an automatic clutch. It offered low-cost motorcycling and therefore sold well.

MAICO 1977 MC400

Dating from the 1930s, this German firm produced road racing and off-road machines in various sizes. This is a typical moto-cross machine built with 247cc, 386cc and 438cc engines. They were powerful machines.

GILERA 1977 125TG1
The 122cc two-stroke engine with a five-speed gearbox of this stylish tourer was used in a trail machine.

TECNOMOTO 1977 MINI CROSS
Typical Italian miniature machine, built for children to capture their interest when very young. This is one of a series of similar models, all powered by a restricted two-stroke moped engine for use in private areas.

MOTO GUZZI 1 979 850 LE MANS II
The Le Mans was the sports version of the classic Guzzi V-twin and offered cockpit fairing, low bars and footrests placed well back on the frame. This provided a comfortable riding position for fast, long-distance journeys.

✿OSSA TRIAL

OSSA 1978 TRIAL
One of the major Spanish firms that became dominant in trials riding during the 1970s along with Bultaco and Montesa. British riders helped develop these machines to a very competitive level, until Japanese manufacturers took the lead, often with the help of the same British riders.

SWM 1978 RS 250 GS
An Italian machine built for enduro events, when the small headlamp would be used. Based on a motocross model, it was a competition machine fitted with lights to make it street-legal, although still fitted with the expansion exhaust. It was used in long and tough races that were hard on the rider as well as the machine.

CAGIVA 1979 SST 250
Set to become a dominant factor in Italian motorcycling, this firm began by taking over the two-strokes being made by Aermacchi for Harley-Davidson. This is one such, there were also 350cc and trial models, but they soon moved on and later acquired Ducati.

SANGLAS 1979 400-Y
Most of the motorcycles from this Spanish firm were solid, dependable four-strokes, built for law enforcement and public agencies. In the 1970s this model joined the range. It used a 392cc Yamaha XS400 engine with single overhead camshaft and six-speed gearbox and Spanish cycle

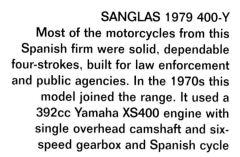

LAMBRETTA 1979 GRAND PRIX
This firm was the other major Italian scooter manufacturer and this model reflects their style very well. The power came from a 148cc or 198cc two-stroke engine, the side panels detached easily for access to the mechanics for maintenance.

DUCATI 1979 500SL PANTAH
A new form of camshaft drive (toothed belt) was introduced with this model. The 499cc engine was soon joined by a 583cc version. This led the way for many other sizes. The camshaft drive system was much cheaper to make and easier to set up than the old shaft and bevels.

DUCATI 1980 900SS
One of the classic Italian motorcycles, the 900 used the desmodromic, or positive, system to control the valves, the overhead camshaft of each cylinder being driven by shaft and bevel gears. A great machine built for distance riding at speed.

FANTIC 1980 CABALLERO
This Italian firm concentrated on small-capacity two-stroke engines fitted to a range of machines for road, trail, enduro or motocross. Most engines were of 50cc or 125cc, but unit built with four-speed or six-speed gearboxes. Aimed at the youth and competition market, they were popular and sold well.

BENELLI 1980 500 QUATTRO
In 1972 Benelli introduced the Sei, a machine that had a transverse-six engine. They followed this with fours of 231cc, 346cc and 498cc capacity. The six and larger fours bore a distinct resemblance to the Honda fours of the time, but the 250cc was a jewel.

SIMSON 1980 KR 51/2
This is another product of the East German MZ plant. The mopeds and light scooters were sold under the Simson label. This scooter has a 50cc two-stroke engine with the choice of a three-speed or four-speed gearbox. The latter also had a version with electronic ignition.

BMW 1980 R80G/S
The firm's first trail machine which was the start of a series of models in a similar style. Rather heavy for off-road use, it made a light and useful road model and proved very popular.

VESPA 1980 P125X, P150X & P200E
The new line from Piaggio, built in three capacities, all with a four-speed gearbox and common cycle features. The style is still very similar to the 1946 version. Most parts had several jobs to do and this helped to keep the weight low.

VESPA 1980 SI MOPED
A new model, available in Europa and Montecarlo formats with optional suspension systems, transmission, wheels and seats. All used a 49cc two-stroke engine and both forms of transmission were automatic.

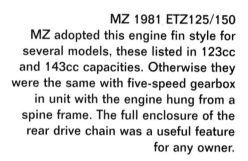

MZ 1981 ETZ125/150
MZ adopted this engine fin style for several models, these listed in 123cc and 143cc capacities. Otherwise they were the same with five-speed gearbox in unit with the engine hung from a spine frame. The full enclosure of the rear drive chain was a useful feature for any owner.

BMW 1985 K100
After building motorcycles with flat-twin engines for 60 years, BMW finally added a new range in the form of the K100 fours. These had the in-line four set along the frame, laid on the side, which gave the gearbox and shaft drive the best position. The sports K100RS was the model that retained the BMW feel and riding style.

BMW 1985 K75C
Once the new fours were launched, BMW added a three-cylinder version in several styles, this one with cockpit fairing. Both threes and fours became known as flying bricks, as a result of the engine shape.

DUCATI 1980 900 REPLICA
Mike Hailwood won the 1978 Formula 1 TT and this Replica model was introduced in the style and colour of his machine the following year. It used the 864cc desmodromic engine in the classic Ducati style and is also referred to as the MHR model.

LAVERDA 1982 JOTA 1000
From their 750cc twin, Laverda developed the 981cc triple. The sports version, the Jota, was capable of over 225 km/140 miles per hour performance with race-winning brakes and handling. This made it one of the quickest road bikes of its time.

SIMSON 1986 S51
ENDURO
This light motorcycle had the
same 50cc two-stroke
engine as the scooter and
was also available with a
three-speed or four-speed
gearbox. Simple and basic,
it was well up to its job, in
this case off-road, with
raised exhaust and high
bars.

SIMSON 1993
A small scooter from the MZ
works that used the 50cc two-
stroke engine and four-speed
transmission. Versions with
optional electric start or
kick-start, drum or disc front
brakes were available.

**TOMOS 1987
AUTOMATIC 3ML**
This make hailed from Yugoslavia, but also had a factory in Holland, a good centre to sell mopeds from. A 49cc two-stroke engine, two-speed automatic gearbox, cast wheels and simple construction made for a good product.

DUCATI 1993 750 SUPERSPORT
The modern Ducati continued to use the desmodromic engine with the belt-driven camshafts, in several sizes with varying degrees of tune and body enclosure. Very successful in World Superbike racing, all the models are highly regarded and most desirable for fast road riding.

MOTO GUZZI 1994 NEVADA 350
This custom model was listed with a choice of V-twin engine in either the usual 744cc or as a smaller 346cc (shown here). In other respects the two machines were essentially the same.

CAGIVA 1995 ELEFANT 900
Cagiva took over the Ducati V-twin engine and used it for their own range, including the off-road machines built in 748cc and 904cc capacities. Well equipped, the larger with six speeds, they were among the best in their class.

MuZ 1995 SAXON TOUR 500
MuZ turned to the Austrian Rotax engine for this model. It had a 494cc ohc four-stroke engine, a far cry from their usual two-strokes, although the same chassis were available with smaller, more basic engines.

APRILIA 1995 RS250
An Italian firm that became famous because of its successful grand prix machines. This stunning model used the most modern technology. A twin-cylinder, two-stroke 249cc engine set in a *V*, six speeds and handling and brakes to match the best completed this quality machine.

PIAGGIO 1995 ZIP & ZIP
A Vespa with a difference because it has a 49cc two-stroke engine and electric motor powered by batteries under the seat. Thus, the rider can switch to zero-pollution and continue in areas barred to conventional vehicles.

BMW 1994 F650
BMW really broke from
tradition with this model,
listed as the Funduro. It
used a 652cc single-
cylinder Rotax from
Austria, built by Aprilia in
Italy, and had chain final
drive. It was intended to
be an entry-level model
for use on or off-road.

PIAGGIO 1995 SKIPPER
This was part of the Vespa
1990s range, fitted with a
123cc two-stroke engine in a
new format. Modern style
ensured that the make
continued to be prominent in
the scooter market.

175

MOTO GUZZI 1995 DAYTONA 1000
Finally, the vulnerable V-twin engine gained four-valve heads and fuel injection for the 992cc to create this model, but kept the general form and shaft drive. This machine could cruise at high speeds and toured over long distances in comfort.

BMW 1995 R1100R
The boxer engine was revamped in 1993, when four-valve heads and fuel injection were introduced alongside the new Telelever suspension system. A trail version was introduced the following year and the 848cc roadster model, shown in this example, the year after that.

LAVERDA 1995 650 SPORT
This firm returned to the market in 1994 with a machine powered by a 688cc twin with four-valve heads, twin overhead camshafts, a six-speed gearbox and covered by this stylish fairing.

177

JAPAN:
THE COLOSSUS

HONDA 1995 CBR600F

T he Japanese motorcycle industry seemingly swept out from nowhere to bear down on Europe and the United States. Unknown to the world in 1960, they were dominant by 1970, as the name 'Honda' became synonymous with 'motorcycle'.

The Japanese industry began in the early 1900s. A handful of machines were imported and the Japanese set out to see how these new devices worked. It led to the first Japanese-built motorcycle in 1908, which was soon followed by others from fledgling firms.

The production and sales volumes were minuscule: a firm named Nihon sold only 20 machines. This was hardly surprising in a country with few roads and where boat travel was the norm. Motorcycling became more popular after the First World War, because it was cheaper than motoring and more suited to the narrow tracks that passed for roads in this still undeveloped country.

However, the imported machines were popular and this almost destroyed the infant manufacturing industry. A few firms survived, buying the more specialist parts such as magnetos or carburettors from abroad, and assembled

HONDA 1952 CUB
Honda's affordable 50cc bicycle attachment put personal transport within the reach of most people's pockets – the guiding philosophy that was to make the company the largest motorcycle manufacturer in the world.

SUZUKI 1953 DIAMOND FREE
Suzuki also started as the maker of small, two-stroke, attachable engines. In 1953, the original 50cc model was enlarged into this 60cc one.

YAMAHA 1955 RED DRAGONFLY
The first Yamaha was this 125cc YA1. It was a copy of the prewar DKW RT125, a model also imitated by BSA, Harley-Davidson and Voskhod.

RIKUO 1955 350 SINGLE
Harley-Davidson licensed production of its V-twin models to the Japanese firm Rikuo in the 1930s. After the war, Rikuo used a BMW design for this machine, but an overhead camshaft made it far from a direct copy.

LILAC 1956 FY-5
From their start in 1948 the Marusho firm, who built the Lilac, concentrated on shaft-drive machines such as this 242cc ohv single with its four-speed gearbox. A three-speed version won the 250cc race at the 1955 Asama meeting.

HONDA 1956 DREAM SA
This 246cc single was the first Honda fitted with an overhead camshaft and was accompanied by a similar 344cc SB model. Both had unit construction of the four-speed gearbox and changed to leading-link front forks the next year.

HOSK 1957 AB
Hosk began by building engines and transmissions in 1946, moving on to complete motorcycles three years later. This 250cc ohv single was one of a four-model range which included a 500cc twin with overhead camshaft.

FUJI 1957 250
This neat model, with many European features, was manufactured by one of the many small firms that the larger companies eventually swallowed up.

SUZUKI 1959 SUZUMOPED
The lines of this 50cc model – its spine frame, short leading-link front forks and pivoted-fork rear suspension – reflect those of 1950s European mopeds. The 1958 model had had belt drive.

HONDA 1959 CB92
This, the sports version of the 125cc twin, had sharper styling than the tourer. Both this model and the similar 250cc twin had an overhead camshaft and four-speed gearbox, allowing the engines to run at speeds unprecedented to European eyes and ears.

SUZUKI 1967 GT500
One of the most underrated machines of all time, this simple, twin-cylinder two-stroke had no looks to attract buyers but was very fast and dead reliable, even in the hottest of climates such as Death Valley, California. Built for eight years, owners loved it despite its vibration and thirst.

KAWASAKI 1964 SG
This 248cc ohv single was based on an older model by Meguro, a firm that built British-style machines during prewar days. Kawasaki took over Meguro and used its designs as a basis for part of their early range.

MARUSHO 1966 MAGNUM
This 500cc flat-twin model was intended for sale in the United States. It proved unreliable and Only 188 were made. The experience showed that building a BMW replica was not an easy task.

KAWASAKI 1966 W1
Meguro-built twins had the style of the BSA Golden Flash and Kawasaki stretched this out to 624cc for this series. While keeping the external shape, the internals were rather different from the British twin. It sold well in Japan, but not in its intended market, the USA.

BRIDGESTONE 1967 GTR350
The twin cylinder, two-stroke engine of this make used the rotary inlet valve, which made for a wide unit. Bridgestone's well-built machines were sold mainly in the United States, until the firm decided to concentrate on tyre production.

them with castings machined locally. Success was limited because they were competing against established firms with more advanced products, while the home manufacturers had to build the machines by hand in a similar way to the early European manufacturers. In addition, the whole concept of spare parts fitted to replace worn ones was simply unknown, so machines were discarded for the want of a simple item.

This changed in 1922 when the government decreed that subsidies would be granted to the makers of vehicles, subject to two provisos – the machines had to be suited for military use and made in Japan. This encouraged larger firms into the market, although several found motorcycle manufacture a much more difficult enterprise than they had first anticipated.

One firm succeeded, manufacturing the Arrowfast. This bike had a 633cc side-valve engine, three-speed gearbox, reverse gear for sidecar use, girder front forks and electric lighting. There was also a 250cc version available and hundreds of each were sold, the first mass-produced motorcycle built in Japan. They proved popular even

though the engines were not as good as those found on imported models.

Most imports were either British or American and this dependence on foreign products worried a government increasingly dominated by the military. This escalated at the start of the 1930s as the seeds of Japan's long war with China (1937-45) were sown. The need for machines also increased but measures to halt imports were set aside. The Japanese then bought the manufacturing rights of some machines from Harley-Davidson, who were keen to find a new foreign market because of import tariffs raised by Britain.

Along with the machine drawings, Harley-Davidson also taught the Japanese how to organise factories for the mass production of sophisticated products, about the heat treatment of metals, precision machining and assembly lines. The lessons were not forgotten and were passed on to many other industrial firms throughout Japan.

The Japanese-built Harley was sold as the Rikuo and the army had ordered 18,000 of them by 1945. After war broke out with China, all civilian production of the Rikuo

2 ROTARY VALVES
2 CARBURETORS
5 SPEED GEARBOX
2 ALUMI-CYLINDERS
2 STROKE ENGINE

KAWASAKI 1967 SAMURAI
This 247cc twin-cylinder, two-stroke model with rotary inlet valves was accompanied in the model range by a 338cc, the Avenger, in road and street-scrambler forms. Both offered the fast acceleration vital for sales in the United States, and they established the company name for performance.

*Maui Blue Metallic

SUZUKI 1967 B120
Developed from the 1964 B100, which used the same 119cc two-stroke engine, this simple model ran on for another decade with its basic format and four speeds. It proved a popular choice for riding to work and around the neighbourhood.

HONDA 1968 CB750
Four cylinders, an overhead camshaft, five speeds, disc front brake, electric start and full equipment at an affordable price – Honda's big bike took such machines out of the category of expensive exotica.

SUZUKI 1972 GT750
Built as a grand tourer able to compete with the largest from Honda, Kawasaki and Triumph, the GT750 had a 739cc three-cylinder, water-cooled, two-stroke engine and was known as either the kettle or the water buffalo. It had considerable success on the racetrack.

and other makes such as Meguro, Miyata and Cabton ceased.

After 1945 Japan's industry was wrecked and transport virtually nonexistent. The country was under US military occupation and the economic cartels, dominant during the interwar period, had gone. Entrepreneurs were able to seize an opportunity. Soichiro Honda was one of several who bought surplus army engines and bolted them to a bicycle. These machines were crude, basic and only a small numbers were produced, 127 in 1945, 211 in 1946, but 387 motorcycles plus 1623 scooters in 1947 when Japan exported a total of 10 machines.

Most of the machines were built using scrap, especially from aircraft, so Nakajima's Rabbit scooter had a body made from light-alloy panels and used tail wheels from bombers. Desperate measures they may seem, but in time the firm developed into the industrial giant, Subaru.

Many of the designs were too large, heavy and expensive for the time. Most people could only afford a small engine to add to their bicycle. This led to firms just building these units, as in Europe, and the numbers of complete motorcycles produced remained low until 1951.

Then expansion began and the number of firms multiplied to around a hundred. Most were small and began by copying existing designs from wherever they could find the information. The first half of the 1950s saw production rise from a few thousand to over 200,000 as firms were encouraged to produce machines for the home market, which the government ensured was protected.

They did this by various means, first by imposing a 40 per cent import duty in 1952. All the official agencies such as the police and postal services were instructed to buy only Japanese and then, in 1955, currency controls were inposed on private citizens. No longer could they change their yen into pounds, dollars, marks or lire. It became illegal to export yen. The choice of consumers was restricted to a Japanese machine or to walk. This created a captive home market.

At the same time the firms were encouraged to scrutinise foreign products. They could import them for this purpose without paying either duty or tax, and were even offered cheap loans for the purpose. This led to a number of nearly exact copies of European machines with DSK copying the BMW R50 model, in spite of a protest by the

SUZUKI 1972 GT380
As well as the big triple GT750, Suzuki also built two smaller, air-cooled threes, this GT380 and the GT550. Both had similar styling, most noticeably the cast shield over the cylinder heads known as ram-air-cooling.

187

YAMAHA 1973 RD250
The firm introduced twin-cylinder two-strokes to its range as early as 1957 and by the 1970s were offering the RD models in 125cc, 200cc, 250cc, 350cc and then 400cc capacities. Similar in design, all offered high performance and this RD250 reflected the advances made since they began.

German embassy. Sangyo copied the Sunbeam in-line twin, Honda the NSU and Yamaha the Adler and DKW.

This trend did not last long, but a curious result was that the firms that copied German and Italian designs survived, while those that had copied the British did not. Firms in the first two countries were still innovative, while those of the third coasted on past glories.

During this period Honda and the other manufacturers bought the latest machine tools for their factories and were able to undercut their rivals. Honda introduced the powered wheeled Cub, in 1952, this easily fitted on any bicycle rear wheel and soon accounted for 70 per cent of Japanese motorcycle production.

Small firms had little chance of competing against this and were ruthlessly put out of business. Designers were therefore forced to move from firm to firm and quickly built up knowledge of what worked well and, more importantly, what did not. In time this paid great dividends.

Technical progress was pushed further as a result of racing events held at Mt. Asama, the first in 1955. Prior to that there had been only isolated events such as the

Nagoya TT of 1953. Asama was set up to force on the pace of development, and it was a rule that every part of a competing machine had to be made in Japan. No Renolds chains or Dunlop tyres from England, Bosch electrics from Germany or Dell'Orto carburettors from Italy, because the aim was to improve Japanese technology.

The Asama circuit curled around the slopes of the mountain, the track surface a mixture of dirt, volcanic ash and gravel. The first meeting showed that Japanese manufacturers had a great deal to learn from the technically more advanced Europeans, but they returned in 1957 in better form. A Clubman race where foreign machines could compete was held at the circuit the following year. They did so successfully in the larger classes and the feat was repeated in 1959. However, it was then that the world first saw the racing Honda fours, a sure indication of the company's direction.

The second half of the decade saw the Japanese industry reduced to eight major firms. Some had amalgamated, others simply folded. Honda remained the industry leader. The total Japanese industry production volume increased to 250,000 in 1956, and 750,000 in 1959. That was the year Honda first raced in the TT, and a year after they had introduced their Super Cub scooterette, the model that sold over 20 million units, breaking all production records.

In 1960 Japanese production exceeded 1.3 million yet they exported only 52,000 machines. The rest of the world just did not realise that Japan had the best factories, best machine tools and the ability to grind out machines at an astonishing rate. In addition, the home market was saturated and they now needed to export most of their production. To achieve this they sought publicity and advertising to reach new market sectors.

Road racing was the field in which they chose to demonstrate their abilities, but at first they had limited success. After their visit to the TT in 1959, Honda ventured back in 1960 with 125cc twins and 250cc fours which were more competitive. In 1961 they won most of the 125cc classics and all but one of the 250cc events.

In 1962, Honda's domination spread to the 350cc class, but their efforts in the new 50cc classics were thwarted by Suzuki, to whom East German, Ernst Degner had defected, along with his knowledge of the MZ two-stroke. This was to be taken and developed by all the Japanese firms to unprecedented power outputs. From 1962 to 1967 Honda, Suzuki and Yamaha raced with ever more complex machines, sharing most of the honours. Honda exploited the four-stroke engine with twin camshafts and four valves per cylinder, the others used disc-valve two-strokes. Engines with one, two, four, five or six cylinders came from Japan. These were able to run at incredible speeds, and called for up to twelve gears for the smallest.

Even more complex models remained in the experimental shops at the factories.

It was a wonderful time for spectators, but extremely expensive for companies. Having demonstrated their expertise, the factory teams withdrew from competition. With the publicity generated from racing, the firms, Honda in the lead, established themselves in world markets offering clean, reliable and sophisticated road models. Their handling might not have been on a par with the best from Europe, but their electrics were far better and their performance far above the standard of the day.

They sold in vast numbers and expanded the market. The manufacturers initially concentrated on the small-capacity, high sales end of the spectrum. By the mid-1960s Japan was producing over 2 million machines a year, and their larger machines soon began to appear at the top end of the showroom.

As the 1970s progressed more exotic models came from Japan; the three major firms – Honda, Suzuki and Yamaha – were joined by Kawasaki in 1962. The factories returned to road racing, running in events in America as well as the grand prix circuit, plus endurance and long-distance races. In these they were successful, just as they were in off-road events once they got involved.

Around 1980, the Japanese solved the handling problems of machines that had outgrown their earlier designs. The combination of massive power and modest tyre widths had lagged behind US and European products, and many were a handful to drive. After 1980 this problem receded, even if some machines were ridden harder to find new limits.

HODAKA 1973 COMBAT WOMBAT Aimed at the USA market, hence the model name, this was one of a series of off-road and competition models built in Japan and sold from a distributor in Oregon during the 1970s.

YAMAHA 1973 FS1E
Known to thousands of teenagers as Fizzie, this 50cc two-stroke was the sports moped that most began their riding days on. At that time the pedals were required by the law in some countries, but they folded back to give a good riding stance.

HONDA 1973 CD175
For just over a decade this model, launched in 1967, was a best seller to commuters. For riders who needed a little more than the Supercub could offer, here was a machine with twin cylinders, overhead camshaft, four speeds and the right blend of performance and economy.

However, the market shrank in the 1980s as the companies began to concentrate on two model lines. One was the race replica, the other the large-capacity trail model, both of which were designed as copies of factory machines down to their line and paint finish. While continuing these trends and using some very high grade technology in the process, the manufacturers did not drop their practice of changing many of their models on an annual basis. Motorcyclists gradually began to react against the resultant high costs of spares.

This situation became worse as both model types adopted fairings and other vulnerable parts. It soon became expensive to allow a machine to fall over, even a trail model which could be expected to be dropped often when off-road.

It led to difficult times in the 1990s when the retro style was added to the other model lines. This proved popular and helped to relieve the situation, but it was not until the mid-1990s that Japanese manufacturers slowed down the model changes. Most of the alterations were directed at the large machines, because the small, more basic models had very long production runs – changing them would be extremely costly. Only the graphics, panel finishes and

SUZUKI 1974 SCOOTERETTE
The first scooterette produced by Suzuki was the M30 model, released in 1963. In 1969 they produced the F50 and the larger F70, which became known as the FR70 in 1974.

tanks were changed – the engine unit and chassis would remain unaltered for many years.

In the future the long production run is to apply to the entire range and there is to be greater concentration on basic transport.

HONDA 1974 CB400F
A Honda classic which proved most popular, being compact, fast, well-styled thanks to the four exhaust pipes all running to one side, and a good handler. Similar to an earlier CB350, it was of 408cc capacity and followed the form of the CB750 but with six gears.

YAMAHA 1975 TY250
A pure trials model was listed by Yamaha for many years and this is typical of the type during the 1970s. Later models had a water-cooled engine and monoshock rear suspension along with many detail changes and improvements.

KAWASAKI 1976 KH100
For many a year the firm built models such as this in several sizes and forms, but the engine unit stayed as it was right through into the 1990s. A simple two-stroke with rotary inlet valve in unit with a five-speed gearbox, it performed well and served commuters well.

KAWASAKI 1977 Z200
In effect, this 198cc single was half a 400cc overhead camshaft twin, and was produced for the commuter market for riders who preferred a four-stroke for their ride to work. It used a five-speed gearbox and was well fitted out for its task.

YAMAHA 1976 XT500
This big four-stroke was aimed at the trail market but performed better on the tarmac where its 499cc carried it along with style. Rather tall and heavy for off-road work, it was soon joined by a pure road version, the SR500. Later it was enlarged and went to a four-valve head.

YAMAHA 1977 XS400
One of a family of overhead camshaft twins which appeared in the mid-1970s as the firm extended its model range to include four-strokes. Typical of the time, it had six speeds, electric start, disc brakes and cast-alloy wheels.

YAMAHA 1975 XS650
The XS650 was originally launched in 1972 as the XS2. It was an attempt to capitalise on the success of the British vertical twins by offering an overhead camshaft and five speeds.

KAWASAKI 1975 MACH IV
In 1968 the firm introduced the H1 model with its 499cc three-cylinder, two-stroke engine, dynamic performance – and twitchy handling. An instant success, it was soon joined by others including this 748cc version capable of some 200 kilometres /126miles per hour, and 12-second standing quarters. There were also racing versions.

KAWASAKI 1977 Z1000
Late in 1972 the firm launched the Z1, a 903cc four-cylinder four-stroke machine having twin overhead camshafts. It was soon christened 'King of the Road' and was enlarged to 1015cc for 1977 to retain the name for many years.

KAWASAKI 1977 Z750
The firm used the layout of their four to build this twin which tended to vibrate despite balancers in the crankcase. Otherwise it offered good performance and handling.

YAMAHA 1978 XS1100
Top of the range at the time, this 1101cc twin overhead camshaft, four-cylinder machine poured its power through a five-speed gearbox to the rear wheel via shaft drive. A machine with some bulk but with a reasonable seat height and easy to ride far and fast.

YAMAHA 1978 RD50M
One of the many smaller two-strokes listed by the firm over the years, all of which offered good performance and the style of the times. While their appearance was updated frequently, the engine units remained the same for long periods.

KAWASAKI 1979 Z250
This model was a smaller, 248cc version of the single-camshaft 400cc twin. It used the same style and fittings but had a six-speed gearbox to suit its power band, cast-alloy wheels and disc brakes front and rear. A good performer, it filled a gap in the Kawasaki line.

KAWASAKI 1979 Z1300
Built to compete with the Honda CBX, the Z1300 went over the top with its water-cooled, six-cylinder, twin-camshaft engine but it stayed around for a decade with few alterations. Massive and not a town machine, it could cruise the motorways all day, every day.

HONDA 1979 CB250N
This and the similar CB400N had three-valve heads for their twin cylinders and the stock Honda fitments for the period. The CB400N was a good performer, also available with a two-speed automatic gearbox, but the 250 suffered from weight problems so was dropped before the 400.

HONDA 1978 CBX
Six cylinders, twin overhead camshafts, four valves per cylinder and all the Honda style made the 1047cc CBX a legend, just as the racing sixes of the 1960s had been. Rather wide for hard riding, it offered a great performance with looks that no-one could ignore.

YAMAHA 1980 RD350LC
Elsie to a generation of riders who had moved on from their first Fizzie. The addition of water-cooling made the performance of the RD twins even better, while their excellent handling made them a natural contender and winner on the circuit.

KAWASAKI 1979 Z500
This model introduced a mid-range four which continued the marque line and style in a size that suited many riders. It offered a fine balance between speed and economy, both in fuel consumption and general running costs.

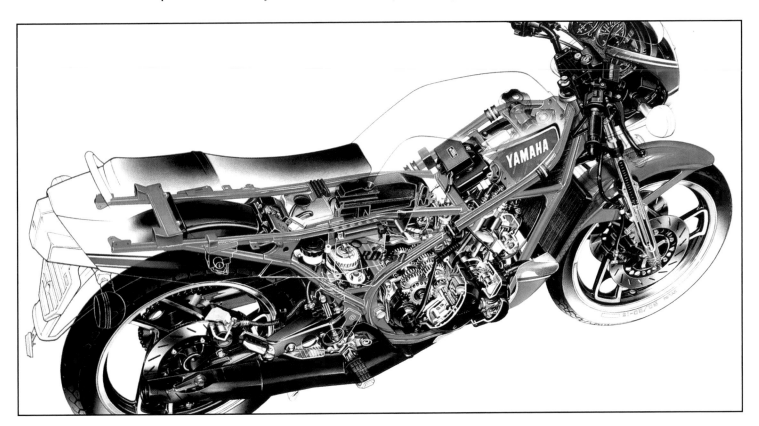

YAMAHA 1980 RD350LC
This cutaway drawing of the larger of the twins shows many of the internal details. This is the machine as in 1983 when the engine was fitted with a power valve and the machine with rear suspension from the motocross range and a belly pan to match the cockpit fairing.

KAWASAKI 1980 Z550
A small gain in capacity enhanced this four although it then became a competitive alternative to Kawasaki's own Z650. Both were able to sell alongside each other in the range for some years.

SUZUKI 1981 GSX1100E
In 1975 Suzuki moved to add four-strokes to their range and began with a four and a twin, both with twin overhead camshafts and very much in the Japanese style of the decade.

KAWASAKI 1981 AR50
Built in 50cc and 80cc sizes and in road or trail forms, this new series brought the style for the smallest machines right up to date with cast-alloy wheels and a cockpit fairing. Two-stroke powered with a reed valve for the inlet and driving a five-speed gearbox, it was the theme for the decade.

KAWASAKI 1981 Z1000LTD
Kawasaki began producing custom versions of their singles, twins and fours as soon as they saw that there was a demand for such a style. This is one of the larger ones, fitted with the usual high bars, stepped seat and special exhausts.

KAWASAKI 1982 GT750
Touring demanded a different approach from the sports market and this model met this with shaft drive and a most comfortable riding posture. A GT550 was added in 1983 and both models became firm favourites with dispatch riders and remained in the lists for many years.

SUZUKI 1981 KATANA
This name heralded a new style for the four-strokes, one that really stood out from the crowd. The GSX1100S and the GSX1000S look very similar, but the larger bike produced a little more power and had a fatter rear tyre.

SUZUKI 1982 XN85 TURBO
The four Japanese firms each tried the turbocharger route to more power, but all found that it added cost and complication without giving any real advantage that could not be easily enough provided by extra capacity. Thus, this 673cc four was no faster than the 1-litre models and was never a strong seller.

KAWASAKI 1981 GPZ1100
This model, and a similar 550, introduced a new sports line to the marque. The machines came with the fairing as standard and were tuned for performance.

KAWASAKI 1982 AR125
A real flyer of a machine, also built in restricted form to suit the British learner market, using a water-cooled two-stroke engine, six-speed gearbox and all the style and fittings demanded by the youth of the 1980s. Quick, with excellent handling.

YAMAHA 1983 XJ900
Effectively replacing the XS1100, this four-cylinder model proved to be an excellent machine destined for a long model life. At first of 853cc it was enlarged to 891cc for 1985.

SUZUKI 1983 GSX550ES
Suzuki here adopted the full-floater rear suspension used by their competition machines. They also added a half fairing and anti-dive forks to update a favourite mid-range model.

HONDA 1984 XL250R
The XL series of trail models fitted with single-cylinder, four-stroke engines began in the early-1970s and remained one of the most popular Honda lines for many years.

Photo: prototype
Foto: prototyp
Photo: prototype
Foto: prototipo

YAMAHA 1984 RD500LC
This machine had a 499cc V-four engine, in effect two RD250s, and had the looks, if not the technology, of the machines taken to world titles by Kenny Roberts. Very quick, but not listed for long.

YAMAHA 1984 FJ1200
This model was launched with a 1097cc twin camshaft, four-cylinder engine but this was enlarged to 1188cc during 1986. A fine sports tourer, it was the model that really established the firm as a serious producer of large four-strokes.

SUZUKI 1984 RM250E
Suzuki won many world motocross titles and incorporated the lessons learned into their production models which ranged in size from 80cc to 500cc. Thus, this model has moved to water-cooling, full-floater rear suspension and other features, all to reduce circuit times.

SUZUKI 1985 CP80
Scooters in 50cc and 80cc capacities continued to be listed, the smaller usually qualifying as a moped with the tax and licence law advantages this gave. This is typical example with a two-stroke engine, automatic transmission and a nice style.

SUZUKI 1990 DR800S
Developed from an earlier and smaller trail model, this version had a massive 779cc single-cylinder engine and other features the firm had used on their rally machines. Twin carburettors fed the twin inlet valves.

HONDA 1985 NS400R
Very much a race replica, this model used a 387cc V-three, two-stroke engine based on that fitted to the successful 1983 works racer, hence the factory-team finish and style for the fairing, tank and seat base.

KAWASAKI 1984
GPZ900R
With this model the firm introduced both water-cooling and four valves per cylinder to its four-stroke range. It set new standards for the class and was all new, being narrower than the first Z1 while including balance shafts in the crankcase to curb the engine vibration.

DVC1 (Dark Violet Cocktail 1)

YAMAHA 1985 V-MAX
A massive 1188cc V-four engine churning out 140bhp made this an awesome performer although many exported machines had a power restriction. Built in a custom style, but more as a cruiser and for drag sprints from traffic lights.

SUZUKI 1985 RG125
Sharply styled for the street and with advanced technology under the fairing, this 123cc model was aimed at the youth market. It was available with full or half fairing and in restricted form to suit learner laws, and matched by similar products from the other Japanese firms.

RED/BLACK

SUZUKI 1986 GSX-R1100
Super sports model with race-replica styling, four-cylinder engine and an aluminium frame. The engine's air-cooling was augmented by internal oil cooling. The front forks were of the inverted, or upside-down, type which were more rigid than the usual layout and became a feature of many machines of the 1990s.

KAWASAKI 1985 GPZ600R
The theme of water-cooling, four-valve heads and fitting a full fairing continued with this and other models, this one from 1990. By then the middleweight class was for 600cc and the Kawasaki was a strong contender.

HONDA 1988 SHADOW
First seen in the United States, but not in Britain until 1992, this custom model used the 583cc V-twin engine but only four speeds in its laid-back chassis which used monoshock rear suspension to give the appearance of a rigid frame.

YAMAHA 1987 TZR250
A further step along the twin two-stroke road came with this model which fitted a redesigned 249cc engine with reed valves into an alloy 'delta-box' frame of a style used by several other Yamaha models. The result was enclosed with a fairing.

SUZUKI 1987 LS650 SAVAGE
This custom model fitted a massive 652cc single-cylinder, four-stroke engine which only needed four ratios in the gearbox. Such an engine size was common at one time and its return revived the notion of simple cruising with few gear changes as the torque pulled the machine and rider along.

YAMAHA 1987 FZX750
A custom cruiser model, based on the race replica FZR750, which kept the 749cc engine with its five valves per cylinder, but installed it in a revised chassis and fitted wheels, seat and other items to suit the style. The petrol tank went under the seat, the one on show being a dummy.

KAWASAKI 1988 VULCAN
The firm had launched a custom 750cc V-twin in 1986 but then came out with this, the VN15 of 1470cc two years later. It had twin camshafts, four-valve heads and shaft drive, but only four speeds as it ran at a modest 4,500rpm.

SUZUKI 1988 GSX600F
Another contender in the mid-range class, offering the best of technology from its four cylinders, 599cc, twin camshafts and 16 valves. Six speeds, full-floater rear suspension, fairing and 'slingshot' carburettors all added up to one very quick motorcycle.

HONDA 1988 REVERE
Listed as the NTV600, this machine used the 583cc V-twin engine fitted into a twin-beam frame with single-sided rear suspension arm. There was shaft drive for Europe, where it was intended to sell to the mature rider, but in the United States it sold as the chain-drive NT650 Hawk.

HONDA 1988 RC30
Also listed as the VFR750R, this was a street-legal racing motorcycle, developed from the factory models and using the V-four engine, aluminium frame and much else from those machines. Internally there was a great deal of high technology and it made a superb road bike and a race winner.

SUZUKI 1989 RGV250
Powered by a 249cc water-cooled, V-twin, two-stroke engine, this model was none too successful in production racing until a revamp for 1991. Even in its early form it still represented some of the best technology available.

YAMAHA 1989 XTZ750 SUPER TÉNÉRÉ
With this model the firm moved from its past to utilise a 749cc slant-angled, twin-cylinder, five-valve engine; in effect half a sports four. This went into an off-road chassis, complete with fairing and the fitments to suit its dual role on and off the road.

SUZUKI 1989 GS500E
This roadster model aimed at adequate performance, economy in fuel and comfort for two in a machine that would be easy to ride on the street. The two cylinders and 487cc were tuned for torque, and the frame and forks set up to suit the style. Brakes, fixtures and fittings were fully modern.

KAWASAKI 1989 KR-1
Water-cooling and many other changes made this twin-cylinder, two-stroke powered model far removed from the Samurai machines of the 1960s. Intended for production racing, the fairing was a standard fitment.

HONDA 1990 GOLD WING
To retrieve lost performance the firm added two cylinders to their old flat-four to produce this 1520cc flat-six. Massive but so smooth, it came fully equipped to offer the height of luxury as a tourer without peer.

SUZUKI 1990 VX800
A roadster in the retro style that became popular in the 1990s, but with a touch of the custom added thanks to the 805cc V-twin engine which, in spite of the appearance of cooling fins on the cylinders, was water-cooled.

SUZUKI 1991 GSX1100G
Further retro-style touring was offered by this large-capacity model which incorporated modern features in its air-cooled, four-cylinder engine in which a balancer shaft curbed the vibration. Shaft drive and five speeds suited its job but the specification did include monoshock rear suspension.

KAWASAKI 1991 KLE500
The trail-machine style began for Kawasaki with the KLR600 of 1984 but this model was intended for road or trail. It used a 498cc twin-cylinder engine having water-cooling and other modern features, but with a 21-inch front wheel to allow it off the highway.

HONDA 1991 NR750
Based on the very advanced technology of the 1979 factory racer, this road model was sophisticated and expensive. It featured a V-four engine with oval cylinders and eight valves for each, twin connecting rods for each piston and much more.

YAMAHA 1991 TDM850
Modelled on the Super Ténéré, this machine retained much of that one's styling and had the engine stretched out to 849cc; but it was not suited to off-road riding owing to a smaller-diameter front wheel.

SUZUKI 1991 GSX-R750W
Suzuki took an established 748cc model, added water-cooling, and released it as a pure race replica. This fine machine feature an aluminium frame, inverted forks, monoshock rear suspension, alloy wheels, full fairing and stylish graphics guaranteed to be noticed.

SUZUKI 1994 RF900R
This model took Suzuki back into the very competitive 900cc class with a super-sports specification. A 937cc four-cylinder, water-cooled engine sat under the sleek fairing along with all the features expected of any such machine in the 1990s. Incredible performance available to all.

HONDA 1991 CR250R
The Honda CR series of competition models dated back to the 1960s when they referred to road-racing models, but during the 1970s began to be used for motocross. Built in a number of sizes, they continued to be listed over the years and reflected the firm's successes in competition with the improvements these brought.

YAMAHA 1992 XJ600S DIVERSION
A combination of an older style for riders returning to motorcycling and the slant-engine lines of the modern sports models but in air-cooled, four-cylinder form for its 599cc. Not exciting but a competent machine.

HONDA 1992 FIREBLADE
Listed as the CB900RR, this model proved to be a top seller and dominated its class. It had a straight-four engine with twin camshafts and four valves per cylinder, water-cooling and six speeds set in an aluminium frame under its race-styled fairing and seat base.

SUZUKI 1991 BANDIT
A sports model that used its lattice-style frame as part of its style and the 398cc water-cooled, four-cylinder engine as a stressed frame member. Thus, it combined something of the retro look with a trend of the 1990s.

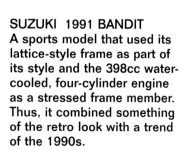

YAMAHA 1993 GTS1000A
Hub-centre steering reappeared for the 1990s with this model which featured Yamaha's Omega chassis. Built as a sports tourer it used the 1002cc five-valve engine in detuned form and was fully equipped with ABS but was both heavy and expensive.

HONDA 1993 BALI
Scooters had always featured in the firm's list and this one used a 49cc two-stroke engine coupled to automatic transmission to move it along. There was storage space under the seat and also in a glove box behind the apron.

HONDA 1992 CB750
The 1990s brought a retro style back into favour, partly as a result of the great interest in classic machines, and Honda produced this transverse four with the looks of the past and air-cooling but with a twin-cam engine and cast-alloy wheels.

YAMAHA 1993 YZF750SP
Built for Superbike racing and based on the very quick sports version, this model varied in having a single seat, larger carburettors and a close-ratio gearbox. Its 749cc five-valve engine was carried in the Deltabox frame and was an impressive performer.

HONDA 1995
GOLD WING & WATSONIAN
Small numbers of sidecar outfits continued to be used in the 1990s. This shows the modern shape available as a contrast to the classic looks of the past. The Gold Wing is hard to better for sidecar work, being fitted with a reverse gear as standard.

HONDA 1994 VFR750F
This super-sports model was introduced in 1986 and went through several major changes to maintain its leading position. It used an advanced V-four, water-cooled engine with 16-valves and twin gear-driven camshafts.

**KAWASAKI 1995
NINJA ZX-6R**
Latest development in the
hyper-sports war with 599cc
water-cooled, twin-camshaft,
four-cylinder, 16-valve engine
in an aluminium perimeter
frame. A high-technology bike
complete with the best in
fixtures and fittings.

YAMAHA 1995 SCOOTERETTE
As with the other firms, Yamaha listed
a step-thru model for year after year.
This one is a 1995 Town Mate with
79cc overhead camshaft engine and
shaft drive.

YAMAHA 1995 ZEST
Scooters continued in the model
range, and this is typical of the
smaller with its 49cc two-stroke
engine and automatic transmission.
Electric start and ease of operation
made such machines a popular
choice for the commuter.